SECRET SCIENCE

THE AMAZING WORLD BEYOND YOUR EYES

DARA Ó BRIAIN

with Sally Morgan
Illustrated by Dan Bramall

Scholastic Children's Books,
Euston House, 24 Eversholt Street,
London NW1 1DB, UK

A division of Scholastic Ltd
London ~ New York ~ Toronto ~ Sydney ~ Auckland
Mexico City ~ New Delhi ~ Hong Kong

Published in the UK by Scholastic Ltd, 2018

Trade hardback edition ISBN 978 1407 18814 0
Scholastic Clubs and Fairs edition ISBN 978 1407 18925 3

Printed and bound in Slovakia

2 4 6 8 10 9 7 5 3

Papers used by Scholastic Children's Books are made from wood grown in sustainable forests.

SECRET SCIENCE
THE AMAZING WORLD BEYOND YOUR EYES
DARA Ó BRIAIN
with Sally Morgan
Illustrated by Dan Bramall
SCHOLASTIC

This book is dedicated to
the Faculty of Science, University College Dublin, who will be surprised I remembered anything.

CONTENTS

Welcome, to your own amazing world!

Yeah, I know. You're looking around at the room you're in and thinking, there's **nothing AMAZING** here. It's **JUST ME** sitting in a chair, or lying on a bed, and there is absolutely nothing exciting occurring.

zzzzZ

Ah! But **AMAZING STUFF is** happening, all around you, all the time. IT'S JUST THAT YOU CAN'T SEE IT.

Look, I'll show you...

Hold the **book** in one hand and **swoop** your other hand through the air. It's a **SIMPLE MOVEMENT**, but when you do it, you disturb **billions** of **molecules** of **air** that are swirling softly around us.

Move your hand **hard enough** and you can make **WIND** and, then if it's above water, **WAVES**.

Move your hand **SHARPLY** enough and you can make a **SOUND WAVE** that makes your ear wobble in and out and your brain can understand as a **noise**.

Put a **MAGNET** in your hand then move it round and everything **electric**, even at the **smallest** level, notices the change, as you alter the sea of **electricity** that's all around us. That sea of electricity carries all the pictures you see with your **EYES**, all the phone calls you make, the radio shows you hear; it can even cook your **DINNER** for you.

Now, take a look at your **HAND**. That's not just you

you're looking at there. There might be more than **3,000 other living things** living on that hand. The **tiniest**, SIMPLEST living creatures, some **USEFUL**, some **DANGEROUS**, but always with us.

Look at the **VEINS** in your hands, **PUMPING BLOOD** all around you, transporting **energy** to all the parts of your body, or carrying messages about **SLEEPING** or **EATING** or **DANGER**.

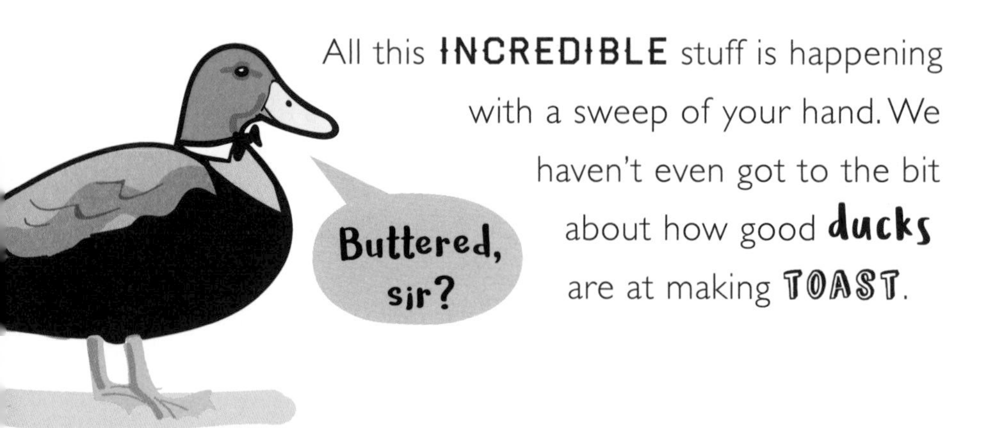

All this **INCREDIBLE** stuff is happening with a sweep of your hand. We haven't even got to the bit about how good **ducks** are at making **TOAST**.

I'll get to that later.

I want to walk you through **a day** of **AMAZING STUFF** that is happening **ALL AROUND YOU**. From when you **WAKE UP** until the moment you go back to **SLEEP**, you walk through a **UNIVERSE** of **forces** and **hormones** and **bacteria** and **electrons** and **waves** and **tastes** and **brain cells** and **pluses** and **minuses** (and how much they LOVE each other).

Yes, I'll get to that later too.

And I want to walk you through all of that and show you just how **AMAZING** your world is and what **BRILLIANT** things are happening all the time without us even noticing.

But first! One word of **WARNING**, and a **GIFT**, and a **PROMISE**.

This book will **bounce** around from one **EXCITING** idea to the next.

I'll show you how you are brought to school by billions of tiny **EXPLODING FISH**.

I'll show you how your **brain** is always ready for a **TIGER ATTACK**, or a **cuddle**, or to collect **gold coins** and finish the next level.

I'll show you why a wave is **not a shark**, and why you **shouldn't** sleep like a GIRAFFE.

And I'll show you these really long words: **sphenopalatine ganglioneuralgia**, and why you **already** know what they mean and are **ALWAYS** willing to risk it happening.

You don't scare me!

I'll tell you about **showering** like an **astronaut**, and why you might find a **COW** in a **laboratory** and why, sometimes, if you sleep longer, you can feel **MORE TIRED**.

I have a **LOAD** of things I want to show you **but** – and this is important – **you might not care about them all.**

Honestly, you might find some of them much less interesting than others.

SO, HERE'S THE GIFT: skip ahead.
If you're reading a bit, **but** it's not your favourite, **JUMP AHEAD.**

You don't want to know why electrons can burp out colours? **That's okay**, you probably want to hear how if your **EYES** and **EARS** don't agree, you'll throw up.

You don't care that a **DEAD BATTERY** is a HAPPY

BATTERY? Fine, you'll probably prefer the **experiment** that involves **eating chocolate**, instead.

Actually, you'll **ALL** want to do the experiment that involves eating **loads of chocolate**. In fact, I might just do that experiment **again** myself **right now.**

Look, you will have your **FAVOURITE** parts and your least favourite parts so... **JUST SKIP AHEAD!**

There's **no test** here, or **HOMEWORK** and at the end of the book I will explain why **skipping bits** is absolutely fine, and probably quite **INTERESTING** in itself.

THAT'S THE PROMISE. I will explain it all at the end, and I just want you to get **there**, okay?

But we have a lot to get through and **ONLY 24 HOURS** to do it all, so, if you're ready...

I'd like to get this day started...

zzzzZ

WOO-HOO! I'M EXCITED! LET'S GO!

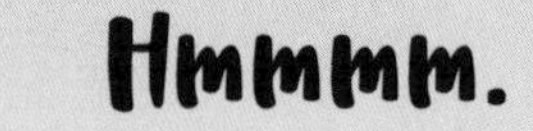

Hmmmm.

I am trying to get this extraordinary day started and you seem to be asleep.

Look at you, in your special pyjamas with pictures of the planets/unicorns/pigs on motorbikes on them, half-in and half-out of the duvet, legs going one way, your head going the other.

What? You didn't know how **SILLY** you looked when you sleep?

Our extraordinary day started just after midnight, but it seems I'm going to be **WAITING** about seven hours until you join me. **BUT WHY?** I mean, your parents are always telling you not to waste time, and yet, every single day you waste about **9, 10, maybe 11** hours of this precious time, conked out and useless. **WHY?**

Most of the BASIC functions we perform every day are pretty obviously useful. We know why we **eat**, **drink**, **wee** and **POO**, for example. Sleep isn't so obvious. For one thing, for most animals (and this includes us, before we started building lovely houses to sleep in) sleep is **DANGEROUS**.

An animal lying down with its eyes **closed** for eight hours makes an easy **snack** for a **BIGGER, HUNGRIER** animal with **SHARP** pointy teeth. In fact, it's so risky that we think giraffes, who live out in the open

on the AFRICAN PLAINS, only nap for about five minutes at a time and until recently, scientists weren't sure if they slept **at all!** Then again, how much sleep do you think you would get, knowing hungry lions were lurking near by?

The lion is the one doing the **EATING** in the savannah, so can afford to be much more relaxed. Lions sleep between 15 and 20 hours every day, sometimes even MORE after a meal. Even your cat at home sleeps about 16 hours a day, presumably so that it is well rested for night-time when it sneaks out of your house to **HUNT** giraffes.

We'll need a ladder...

So, what is so **IMPORTANT** about sleep that animals will put their lives at risk for it? Well, look at these faces:

Scientists puzzled by sleep.

Thanks to **science** there are a lot of things we know for definite, like how fast light travels to Earth from the Sun and what you'll find in the middle of an atom. But there are still **loads** and **LOADS** of things we're not entirely sure about, so you can still catch scientists looking **PUZZLED**. You might think this sounds bad but, actually, it's great. If we knew everything then there would be nothing left to figure out and all the scientists would have nothing to do and they'd sit around all day being **bored** and **UNHAPPY**.

Plus, it means there are loads of things left for **you** to discover later. You've probably already done your first sleep experiment. It's called **'How does it feel when you don't get enough sleep?'** The answer: **ugh, rotten.**

AND IT ONLY GETS WORSE...

In the winter of 1963–64, a brave (and perhaps **FOOL-HARDY**) 17-year-old called **Randy Gardner** from the USA stayed awake for **11 DAYS** and 25 minutes for a school science project. According to Randy, the experiment was fun for the first few days, but **HORRIBLE** from around day four. He started imagining things that weren't happening and at one stage began to believe he was a FAMOUS AMERICAN FOOTBALL PLAYER. By the end of the sixth day, he was having trouble talking and **slurring** his words.

He **SURVIVED**, but Guinness World Records will no longer recognize sleep deprivation attempts because they are too **DANGEROUS**.

Studies done on rats, for example, have shown that if a rat isn't allowed to go to sleep, it will get in a horrible state, with SORES on its paws and tail. A **HAPPY,** well-rested, healthy rat can live for nearly **three years**, whereas one that isn't allowed to sleep **DIES** after just **three weeks**.

So, we clearly **NEED** sleep. **But what is actually happening?**

Well, it seems to be mainly about the **BRAIN**. After all, even if you haven't lifted a finger all day (I'm thinking of **Christmas Day**, say, just **lounging** about eating selection boxes and watching the telly), you'll still need to sleep at the **USUAL TIME**. So, it's about your brain being tired, not your body. But how do we see what's happening in your brain?

Brilliant brainwaves

Your brain is made up of **billions** of nerve cells called NEURONS and they communicate with each other by firing electrical pulses. By communicating with each other, they can do all the **JOBS** your brain does, keeping you breathing, digesting your food, making you run safely down the stairs, REMEMBERING where you put your coat when your mum says, **"Where did you put your coat?"**

We can measure these bursts of electrical activity, called **brainwaves** and, luckily for us, we can do it without having to open up somebody's head. Scientists can measure the bursts of electricity, which helps them to see when the brain is most active, and the different ways our brain works.

Studying sleep

For example, after all that **hard** work during the day **(what with the losing of coats and so on)** you might think that your neurons take a bit of downtime while you sleep, but they don't stop **Firing** at night. In fact, the way we sleep is a lot more **COMPLICATED** than just **Get Tired–Go To Sleep–Wake Up.**

For a start, there are **four different phases of sleep**, and you go through each phase in turn, over and over in cycles, as the night progresses. Different things are happening in your body and brain during each stage (and waking up from each feels pretty different too).

Phase one – dozing off

This is when you are just **drifting** off to sleep and can be easily woken. Sometimes you might have random muscle twitches, or SPASMS, during this phase of sleep, like your leg **jerking**, Scientists call them 'hypnic jerks' –

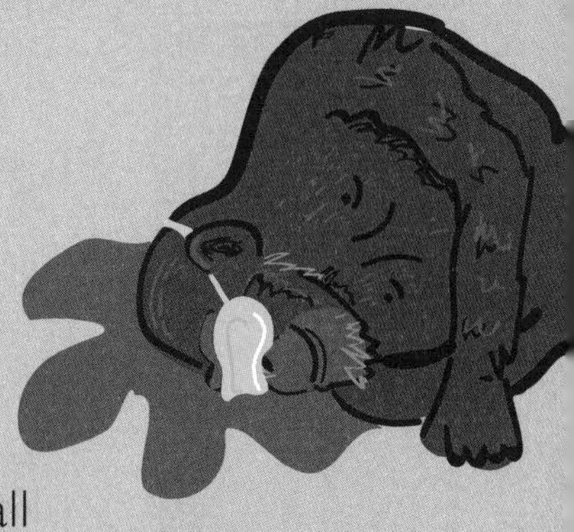

you probably call them **annoying**. There is a theory that this is an old memory in our bodies of when we were **apes** sleeping in **TREES**, and the twitch was to make sure we didn't fall off our branch. I don't say this a lot about science stuff, but even if this wasn't true, I'd tell it to people anyway, because it sounds **AMAZING**. Note: it even happens in bunk beds and you're pretty safe in a bunk bed.

Hypnic jerks even happen in **space**. Astronauts on the **International Space Station** sleep in 'microgravity' as the ship orbits Earth, so to stop themselves **floating** about the space station they sleep in sleeping bags stuck to the wall by velcro. Even though they are constantly **'falling'** some astronauts have reported the same hypnic jerks as they fall asleep, and they are travelling 400kms (240 miles) above the nearest trees.

THIS PHASE LASTS ABOUT 10 MINUTES.

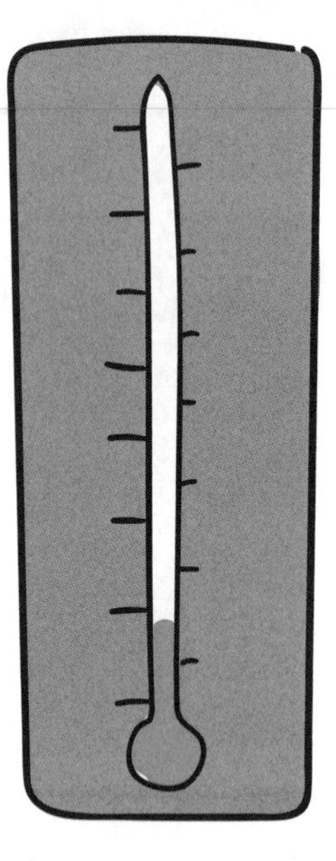

Phase two – light sleep

Your eyes **stop** moving and brainwaves get SLOWER. Your muscles relax further and your **temperature DIPS**. If you are woken during this stage, though you might be **ANNOYED**, it's pretty **EASY** to get up and start your day.

PHASE TWO LASTS FOR ABOUT 20 MINUTES

Phase three – deep sleep

This is where your neurons SLOW down their firing. If there were a **LOUD NOISE** during this stage, you would be **unlikely** to **STIR**. Anyone who wakes you during this bit will be very **UNPOPULAR**. You'll be a right **GROUCH**. And for good reason; you're

DEEP in sleep so that your body can do all sorts of **ESSENTIAL** work. This is the phase of sleep where your body starts to repair muscles, for example, and release **GROWTH** hormones.

THIS PHASE LASTS ABOUT AN HOUR.

Phase four – REM sleep and dreaming

This is the **REALLY STRANGE** one. It's called Rapid Eye Movement **(REM)** sleep, because, well, you can probably guess. This is the part of sleep where DREAMS happen because your mind is active during REM sleep, but your body can't move, or is **PARALYSED**, which is great because it **STOPS** you acting out your dreams. In fact, a picture of your brainwaves during this part of sleep looks just like your brainwaves during the day, apart from the fact you **CAN'T MOVE**.

Scientists think this part of sleep is where your brain sorts out all the **unfinished** business from the day; learning facts, sorting through memories, and generally, if your brain were a computer, tidying up the files on the hard drive and making sure everything gets safely stored away for future use. This may be why you have DREAMS at this stage, as your brain **TIDIES** itself up. We think that RATS and DOGS also dream at a similar stage of sleep, but that they never dream about each other. **(That's a joke; we're not sure what they dream about. They might constantly dream about being each other.)**

EACH CYCLE OF REM SLEEP LASTS ABOUT 90 MINUTES. YOU CAN HAVE UP TO SIX CYCLES OF REM SLEEP EACH NIGHT.

DREAMS are definitely one of those things that need the **CONFUSED** scientist face:

Sigmund Freud, the famous **neurologist** and **psychoanalyst**, believed that dreams hold the key to our hidden **DESIRES**, **THOUGHTS** and **MOTIVATIONS**, and that studying a person's dreams could give you clues as to why they behaved in a certain way. Other scientists believe that even the most **BIZARRE** dreams are just a **biological** process (one that is just a normal, and random, part of life) and is no more useful in understanding why a person behaves the way they do than it is to listen to them **BURP**.

Why do we move around so much in our sleep?

Well, it's not because of our dreams. **SMARTLY**, your body is **unable** to move during your dreams, which is just as well, otherwise you'd **fall** out of bed because you were having a dream about jumping off a **MARSHMALLOW RAFT** into a sea of **ICE CREAM**. We do move **A LOT** when we sleep though, which is why your **duvet** is rarely in the same place at the **END** of the night as it was at the **START**.

Scientists believe you move around in your sleep to **STOP** your body from lying in **one position** all the time. Lying in the **SAME POSITION** for long periods of time **ISN'T GOOD** for you as it stops **blood** from flowing around the body in the way that it should. Pain receptors in the skin sense that your body has been lying in the same spot for **TOO LONG** (a bit

like getting a numb bum) and send signals to your brain to get you to **MOVE** to a more **comfortable** position. Lying in the same position in bed for a single night **probably** won't do you any harm, but staying there longer **ISN'T RECOMMENDED**. Patients in hospital who are unable to move themselves have to be turned in their beds to stop them from getting pressure sores that can become very painful, or even **DANGEROUS**.

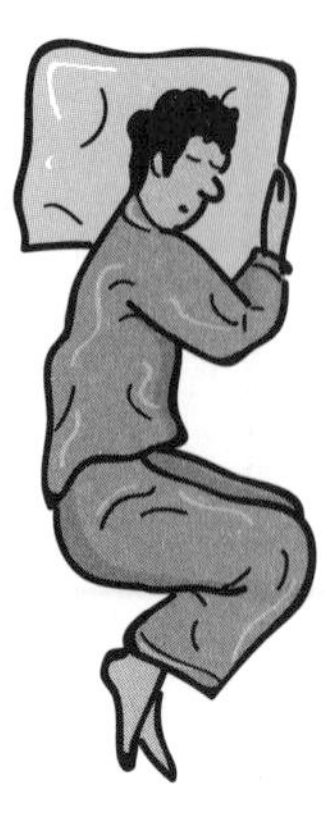

The astronaut **Chris Hadfield**, who lived on the **International Space Station** for six months, said that he slept **VERY WELL** in space (strapped into the special sleeping bag we mentioned earlier). But since he wasn't lying 'on' anything, he didn't roll over or shift at all, and woke up every morning feeling **'STIFF AND CREAKY'** and had to do lots of

STRETCHES to loosen up. But then, he was in

So, time to wake up!

Yes, we really must get this day **started**. We've used up a **THIRD** of it already. **But wait!** What **MOOD** will you be in when you wake up? Well, that's all due to the **phase** of sleep you were in when the **alarm clock** went off.

If you wake during REM sleep, you might take a **few seconds** to shake the idea that you're still on that marshmallow raft, but then your dream will probably **DISAPPEAR** from your memory **FOREVER** in a really infuriating way. **Again, scientists make this face:**

But one of the theories is that dreams occur while the brain is doing various jobs, including **'laying down'** long-term memories of the day before, and so the DREAM itself only gets as far as our **short-term** memory and therefore FADES away quite quickly. With **NIGHTMARES**, this is a good thing.

HOWEVER, if you wake during the **DEEPEST** phase of sleep, **phase 3**, you might not feel great at all. You might feel **GROGGY** and **SLOW** and as if your brain really hasn't got the **WAKE-UP** message yet.

This is called **'SLEEP INERTIA'** and it has a definite effect of SLOWING down your brain. Your reaction times will be slower **(so, no driving the family car for you)** and worse of all, your ability to do abstract brain things like **MATHS** will suffer. The next time you feel really tired after you wake up, **TRY doing some hard sums** and see how you do. *Actually, that doesn't sound like fun.* Okay, do this instead: the next time your mum or dad have a hard time waking up, try **YELLING** some hard sums at them and see how they do. If they get them wrong **(likely)**, you can tell them that it's due to **SLEEP INERTIA** and they will be thrilled at your having educated them **(highly unlikely)**.

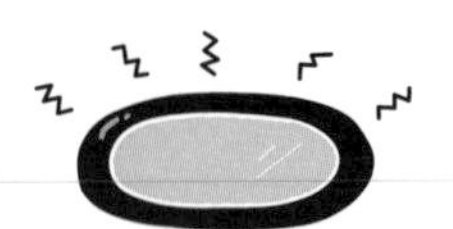

Oh no! You woke up during phase three. What now?

Knowing that you feel so dreadful for a **VALID scientific reason** isn't very comforting but, thankfully, science does have a **SOLUTION**, and no, it does **NOT** involve pressing **'SNOOZE'** on your alarm. What you need is **LIGHT**, so get up and open the curtains or switch on your lamp.

In your brain, there is an awesome thing called the **'suprachiasmatic nucleus'**, or SCN, found deep inside your brain behind your eyes. It controls your sleep cycle by making a chemical messenger for the body, or hormone, called **melatonin**. Hormones are chemicals our body releases to start and stop different processes. Melatonin is the hormone that signals to

your brain that it should sleep. By getting up, opening the curtains or **SWITCHING ON A LIGHT**, you are telling your brain, **"LOOK, THE SUN IS UP! IT'S A NEW DAY!"** and your brain will react by **NOT** releasing any more melatonin and you should wake up more QUICKLY.

Go on. Try it. Shine some light on your suprachiasmatic nucleus and let's get this day going!

It's a new day!

Let's look in the mirror and... **ARGH! WHAT'S WRONG WITH YOUR HAIR?!**

You didn't go to bed looking like that. Now your hair's all shmussed up and wild and pointing in 19 different directions like some giant monster crept into your room and deliberately messed it up.

Well, it **WASN'T** a giant **MONSTER**, it was a tiny, tiny thing, almost the tiniest thing we know. Your hair was messed up by... **ELECTRONS**. Teeny tiny electrons that hate you and want to make you look silly.

What have you done to make the electrons so angry?! AND WHAT ARE ELECTRONS ANYWAY?

To understand electrons, we need to think about what everything is made of. If we look REALLY **CLOSELY** at everything in the world: your hair, my chair, your friend Barry's teddy bear, **EVERYTHING**, it's all made of **ATOMS**.

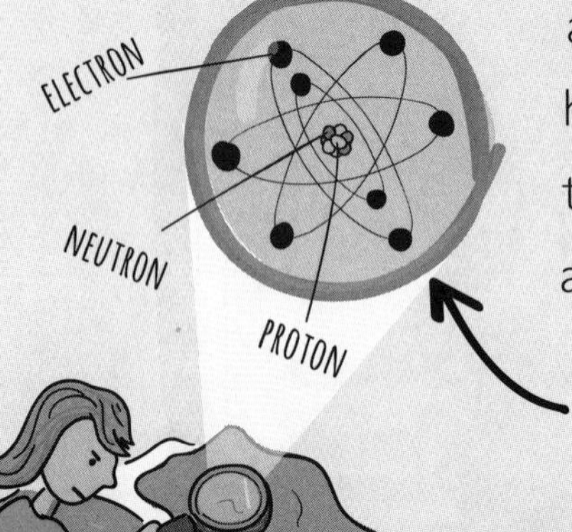

AN ATOM, TA-DAH!

There are **LOTS** of different types of atoms, called '**ELEMENTS**', and they can behave very differently to each other **(some will be** LIGHT, **some HEAVY, some METAL, some** GAS **and so on. We even have a table of them, like a guide to the animals in a zoo, called the periodic table).**

H																	He
Li	Be											B	C	N	O	F	Ne
Na	Mg											Al	Si	P	S	Cl	Ar
K	Ca	Sc	Ti	V	Cr	Mn	Fe	Co	Ni	Cu	Zn	Ga	Ge	As	Se	Br	Kr
Rb	Sr	Y	Zr	Nb	Mo	Tc	Ru	Rh	Pd	Ag	Cd	In	Sn	Sb	Te	I	Xe
Cs	Ba		Hf	Ta	W	Re	Os	Ir	Pt	Au	Hg	Tl	Pb	Bi	Po	At	Rn
Fr	Ra		Rf	Db	Sg	Bh	Hs	Mt	Ds	Rg	Cn	Nh	Fl	Mc	Lv	Ts	Og

La	Ce	Pr	Nd	Pm	Sm	Eu	Gd	Tb	Dy	Ho	Er	Tm	Yb	Lu
Ac	Th	Pa	U	Np	Pu	Am	Cm	Bk	Cf	Es	Fm	Md	No	Lr

Some elements have really famous names like **hydrogen**, **gold** and **mercury**, and most of the rest have similar, and slightly silly-sounding names like **francium** and **caesium** and **californium**.

Sometimes, atoms will be on their own, but they can also link up together to become a thing called a **'MOLECULE'**, and the molecules make up all the many and varied things in the world **(cheese, dog teeth, tinfoil, carpet, basically all the STUFF)**. Molecules have very official sounding names like:

POLY-WOLLY-HYDRO-SHOLLY-DENZO-LENZO-BENZOATE.

That's not a real molecule. But they **OFTEN** have **L O N G**, **RIDICULOUS**-sounding names.

SMIRA-GYRA-PANTSONFIRA-FLOURA-BLOURA-ANTHRAPAZINE.

Again, not a real molecule.

And whenever you hear a grown-up say, **"There are soooo many chemicals in this!"** while looking at a packet of sweets, just **roll your eyes**.

Everything is made of chemicals. Things that are **BAD** for you, things that are **GOOD** for you, things you sit on, things you find up your nose. And these chemicals are made of **molecules**, which are all made of **ATOMS**.

So, it all comes down to atoms. They are the **BRICKS** that **OUR WORLD** is built with.

And all atoms have **roughly** the same shape: there is a bit in the middle and a **'CLOUD'** floating around it. In the middle are the **heavy** bits, two types of particle called the **'proton'** and **'neutron'**, that sit like a cluster of **MARBLES** in a bag. And in the cloud outside of them, all light and fast, float the **electrons**, your hair's arch enemy.

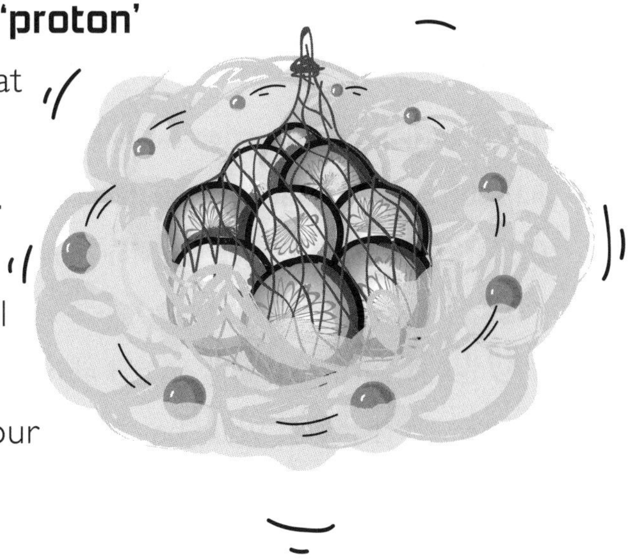

The **PROTONS** have a **positive** electric charge and the **ELECTRONS** have a **negative** charge and that PULLS them together like magnets. Most atoms exist in **perfect balance**, with the same number of protons and electrons, with all the positive and negative charges **cancelling** each other out.

(Not to complicate things too much, but even these teeny protons and neutrons are made of other teenier, tinier things, called 'QUARKS'. But let's leave that for now, shall we?)

YOUR HAIR! We'd almost forgotten! What's this got to do with your hair?

Well, when left alone, the atoms that make up your hair and your pillow are usually pretty **well-behaved**. Your hair behaves, your pillowcase stays **PUT**. All is fine. The atoms, like most atoms, have **NO CHARGE**, all the protons and electrons are balanced out.

Then you went to sleep and as you were **TOSSING** and **TURNING** (trying to keep your body from settling for too long, remember?) you were constantly **RUBBING** your head on the pillow. And by doing that, **believe it or not**, you rubbed some of the **electrons** that were on the **molecules** of your hair onto the **molecules** of the pillow! For some materials, **LIKE HAIR**, the **electrons** in the outer part of their cloud are quite **LOOSELY** held, and rubbing against the right kind of material can dislodge them.

Now you have hair which is MISSING **electrons**, so the strands aren't electrically balanced any more. They lost **electrons**, which are **negative**, so the strands are now **positively** charged and when two things are the same charge, they don't attract each other any more, they **PUSH** each other away.

A bit like this...

So, you have **BAD HAIR** in the morning because you **RUBBED electrons** off it! They are **teeny tiny** things and now they've gone and your hair is a **MESS**.

You might be thinking now, **WAIT!** My head has gone all **positive**, so the pillow must have gone **negative** **(because that's where the electrons went)**. And **positive** and **negative** attract each other! So **THAT'S** why I couldn't get my head off the pillow this morning!

Sadly not. The force of attraction is really, really FAINT. It'll push hair strands apart, but not glue your entire head to a pillow. **SORRY!** You need a BETTER EXCUSE.

You need to sort out that hair. Also, you **SMELL** a bit **BAD**. **Time to hit the shower.**

Go and have a wash

If you are still feeling a bit **GROGGY**, nothing is more **REFRESHING** than a nice shower. But let's all ask the question a scientist would:

Do you really need to?

Firstly, how often do you shower? Well that depends on **where** in the world you live. A study in which lots of people were asked personal questions about their **HYGIENE** habits gave some **FASCINATING** insights into bathrooms around the world.

For instance, the residents of **BRAZIL** and **COLUMBIA** shower **more** than anyone else in the world, with many people showering **more** than once

per day. The **average** for worldwide showering is **seven times a week** and the British come in below that, showering on average **five times a week**. **YUCK!** I hear you say. Well not really, because most scientists **AGREE** that even *that* is probably too much.

Unless your bed is actually the floor of a **MUDDY CAVE**, you probably only really need to shower **once** or **twice** a week. After all, we never see animals having a shower or washing themselves! Apart from **CATS** of course, who might spend up to half their day **GROOMING** themselves and other cats. And **CHIMPANZEES**, one of our closest relatives in the animal kingdom, will often be found **GROOMING** each other and picking **DEBRIS** from each other's hair. The **FISH** of the pacific coral reefs have it well

sussed. There is a species of fish called the **cleaner wrasse** who spend their days **INSIDE THE MOUTHS** of other larger fish, **EATING** the parasites and debris off their teeth!

Right, fair enough, animals clean themselves and in loads of different ways. **But why do we need to wash?**

Well, blame your skin.

The parts of your body that have very specific jobs, like your **heart** or your **lungs**, are called **'ORGANS'**.

Skin is the **BIGGEST** organ of your body. One of its jobs is to **STOP** all of the important stuff in your body from getting out, and to keep nasty things like **bacteria** from getting in. It's important to look after your skin, but at the same time, it actually does a pretty **good job** of looking after itself.

If you take a **CLOSE** look at your skin, you will see lots of little **HOLES**, or 'pores'. Skin releases an oil, called **'sebum'**, from your pores. Sebum coats your skin and makes it **WATERPROOF**.

Too much sebum on your skin can make it look and feel **GREASY** and can combine with **SWEAT** and **DEAD SKIN CELLS** to make excellent food for bacteria and that can make you a little... **SMELLY**.

Great, so now you have **INVISIBLE electrons** messing up your hair and **INVISIBLE BACTERIA** making you **PONG**...

You could wash with just **water** and that will clean away **dirt**, **ink**, **food** and the **salt** from your sweat **(wow, how messy are you?)** but the **sebum**, being WATERPROOF, needs a little more **ENCOURAGEMENT**. And to see why, we have to look right down to the **ATOMS** again.

You probably know the **scientific** name for water, right? It's called **'H_2O'**, because water molecules are made up of **two hydrogen atoms** (the H_2 bit) and one **oxygen atom** (the O bit). The way they link up shares out the **electrons** between them and it leaves the **hydrogen** parts with a **positive** charge and the **oxygen** bit with a **negative** charge. The upshot of this

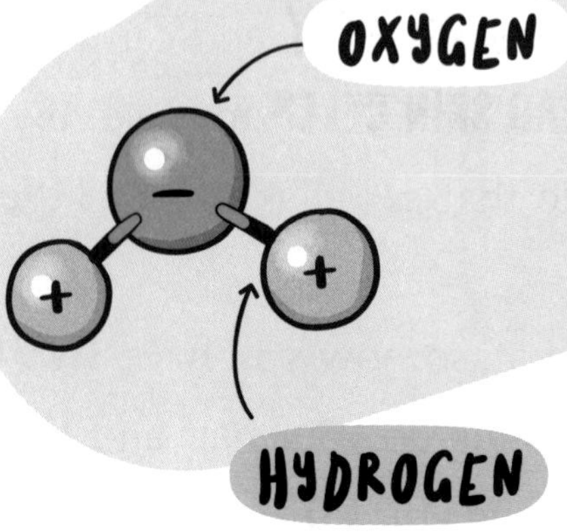

OXYGEN

HYDROGEN

is that water is **'polar'**, that is to say, it's little bit **NEGATIVE** on one side, and a little bit **POSITIVE** on the other.

The **plus** side of a **molecule** likes to be near the minus side of another molecule. This means that when you have **LOADS** of water molecules, like in a **DROP OF WATER**, they all like to **CLING** together because all the pluses and minuses find other pluses and minuses to **JOIN UP** with. Polar things like to mix with other polar things.

This is not EXACTLY what I meant.

SEBUM, and other oils, are **NOT** polar. They have no pluses and minuses. They have no desire to **mix** with water. Water **can't** attract them at all. In fact, if you pour water onto a **GREASY, OILY** surface, like a plate after you've eaten **SAUSAGES**, or the coat of a **PENGUIN**, the water will just run off. **Try it.** But first, find some **COOKED SAUSAGES**, and make friends with a **PENGUIN**. Maybe offer him some **SAUSAGES**.

Anyway, this is where soap comes in.

SOAP is **really**, **REALLY CLEVER**.

Soap is made of really, really long **molecules** that are polar at one end and not polar at the other. One end **ATTRACTS WATER** and the other end **ATTRACTS**, or grabs onto, **OIL** and **GREASE**. Soap basically lifts the **DIRT** from your skin and then gets **WASHED** away with all the **WATER!**

This is true for soap, for shampoo, for washing-up liquid and for the detergent in your washing machine. They all work the same way.

CLEVER

But soap is even smarter than that!

When **SOAP molecules** mix with **WATER molecules**, the **I-love-water-more-than-anything** ends of the **SOAP molecules** grab hold of the **WATER molecules**, while the **I-HATE-WATER** end of the **SOAP molecules** do **EVERYTHING** they can to get **AWAY**. This makes the water separate into **LAYERS**. When **AIR** gets between the layers you get …

BUBBLES!

What you're looking at when you see a **BUBBLE** is **AIR** trapped in a thin layer of **WATER molecules** **squashed** between two layers of **SOAP molecules**. And **POP!** It's gone.

Smile!

All right, time to **BRUSH YOUR TEETH**. **You know why you have to do this.**

You do this because your **PARENTS** keep **telling** you to do this. **Constantly.** At least **twice a day**.

And then the dentist says it, too.

Yes, you brush your teeth because it will keep your **PARENTS** quiet and that is good for your **EAR HEALTH**.

Brushing your teeth keeps your **EARS** healthy and strong and **not over-used** listening to your parents **NAG** you about your teeth.

But, could there be another reason?

We've spoken about a few things **INVISIBLE** to the naked eye already – **electrons** in the atoms, **neurons** in the brain and the surprisingly **BIG** way these little things affect you. Here's another one – **BACTERIA**.

Bacteria – Our tiny friend! And enemy!

Bacteria are tiny **LIVING organisms**, so small you can only see them under a **microscope**. They are not to be confused with **bateria**, which is a type of **BRAZILIAN DRUMMING BAND** that plays samba music. A bateria can be pretty **HUGE**, and when they're doing their thing people start **dancing** and **swaying**. **Bacteria** are tiny and some of them like to **EAT** at your teeth, making them weaker. A **bateria** will never attack your teeth because they're **TOO BIG** to fit in your mouth. They are, after all, **GIANT DRUMMING BANDS**.

So, let's focus on the **bacteria**. Bacteria are teeny tiny little creatures, one of the SIMPLEST forms of life, and they are found just about **EVERYWHERE** on the planet. In the **SEAS**, in the **SNOW**, up your nose, **EVERYWHERE**. There are all sorts of

different bacteria in parts of your body, some doing really **HELPFUL** things, like helping to break down the **FOOD** in your tummy; and others, like the ones in your **mouth**, being really **UNHELPFUL**.

'PLAQUE' is a sticky film made up of bacteria and sugar and it builds up on your **TEETH**, and eats away at the **enamel**, the hard white surface of the teeth. This eventually causes holes called **'CAVITIES'**, or dental caries. The bacteria can also eat away at your gums and cause gum **DISEASE**, which eventually **loosens** your teeth and might even make them fall out. All these are problems the **DENTIST** has to patch up, so we should try to **AVOID** that, really.

We **BRUSH** to get rid of the **PLAQUE** and also to **dislodge** any last bits of food from our meals.

What about toothpaste? What's in that?

TOOTHPASTE is made up of different things all doing different jobs.

Here goes:

There are **abrasives**, which are FINE PARTICLES (a bit like sand, but tinier) that work with your toothbrush to **SCRATCH** the **PLAQUE** off your teeth.

Toothpaste contains **FLAVOURINGS** and **COLOURINGS** that make you actually want to put it into your mouth. **Yummm! MINTY!**

It also contains **chemicals** called **'humectants'**, which is a big fancy word for anything that **ATTRACTS WATER** and so keeps the **TOOTHPASTE** from **SETTING** and going **HARD**. They only work when the **toothpaste lid** is replaced after you use it.

And last but not least...

FABULOUS FLUORIDE!

When **bacteria** start **munching** on the lovely sugar and food coating on your **TEETH**, they produce **ACID** and **ACID** isn't very good for teeth. Enamel, the hard surface of your teeth, is made of minerals, such as **CALCIUM**, and acids love to PULL calcium out of your teeth (this is called 'demineralization'). Demineralization **weakens** the enamel and can lead to **CAVITIES** and this is where **fluoride** comes in. **Fluoride** helps to put the minerals back into your **enamel** or **REMINERALIZE** it, which **HARDENS** the surface of your teeth making them more **RESISTANT** to decay. Phew.

But wait! I didn't eat a meal while I was asleep! **So, why do I need to brush in the morning?**

Well there are TWO good reasons.

Firstly, while you sleep, you produce less saliva **(SPIT)** in your mouth, basically so that you don't **drool** all over your pillow. During the day, your body uses saliva to **MOISTEN** the food you eat and also to start to break it down. It also acts as a **POWERFUL GERM-KILLER** that controls the growth of bacteria in your mouth.

At night, when there is less saliva to get in their way, the **bacteria** in your mouth **MULTIPLY** and you need to clear them away.

Those bacteria aren't **PICKY EATERS** though, so are also happy to feast on the protein found inside your mouth, on your gums and on your tongue.

When the **bacteria** in your mouth eat **PROTEIN** they produce FOUL-SMELLING GASES. Which is why your breath is so **SMELLY** when you wake up. You need to brush your teeth in the morning to help **scrape** away all these **STINKY** midnight-feasting **bacteria** before they eat any more of your mouth.

So, get **BRUSHING**, to get rid of those **NASTY bacteria** and clear out that **STINKY PONG** they left behind. Don't forget to RINSE with lots of **WATER** though. **Fluoride** protects your **teeth**, but it isn't good to swallow **(no matter how yummy the flavour of your toothpaste)**.

So, are we **finally** ready to start the day? It seems that all we've done is wake up and have a **WASH**. And yet, we've explored **electrons** and **molecules**, **neurons** in the **brain** and **bacteria** in your mouth. Everything we've done has seen some **INVISIBLE** world affecting us, some **tiny** thing **INTERRUPTING** our **HUGE** life, and that is going to **keep** happening all day.

Best have some **BREAKFAST** and get ready to face it.

WE WILL NOT
MENTION POO
DARA

You must be starving by now.

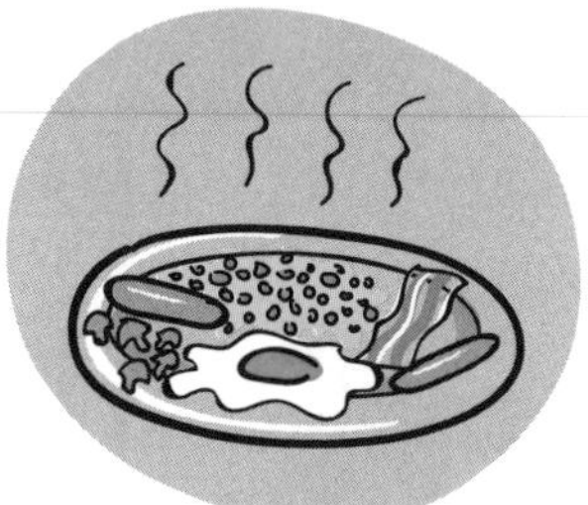

You've probably not eaten since TEA-TIME yesterday and so should be feeling **HUNGRY**. Like all living things, humans need food to **survive**. We extract **energy** and **nutrients** from what we eat and if we haven't done that in a while, your stomach releases a hormone – a chemical messenger called GHRELIN – to your brain, to remind it to **FIND MORE FOOD**.

There are **many** reasons we like to eat food; often it's quite **YUMMY**, we get to sit around a table with our family, it **cheers us up**, **WARMS US**, gives us something to **THROW** at our friends at a party, and so on. Your body is slightly more **BUSINESS-LIKE** about it.

BASICALLY, YOU ARE A FOOD-PROCESSING PLANT.

Your digestive system is a lot like a **conveyor belt** in a **FACTORY**. You put the food in one end, your body gets to work on it, takes what it **needs**, and **DUMPS** the stuff it doesn't need out the other end. Yeah, you know what I mean. Let's not make this all about the **POO**.

FIRST PART of the process: **SMASH IT UP** with your teeth. All the **GRINDING**, **BITING** and **CHEWING** breaks food up into **smaller** pieces so that your body can work with it more easily. Chewing also mixes food with saliva, which adds **MOISTURE** and turns it into a kind of **MUSH**, so it can **MOVE** through your system easily. The saliva also starts to break down the **sugars** in your food, into a form your body can use for **energy**.

You **SWALLOW** your food and it **passes** down a pipe called the **OESOPHAGUS**, to the **next**

stage in the processing plant – **YOUR STOMACH**. This takes about 10 seconds. I say **'down'** because we usually eat **sitting**, or even **standing** up, so it might seem like the food just **FALLS** down to your tummy. **It doesn't though**; if you stood on your head and chewed, you would still be able to **SWALLOW** and the food would go to your stomach, **NOT YOUR BRAIN**. The parcel of **MUSHY FOOD** is carried along the **OESOPHAGUS** by **muscle contractions** (when your muscles work hard – getting shorter and thicker to push the food down).

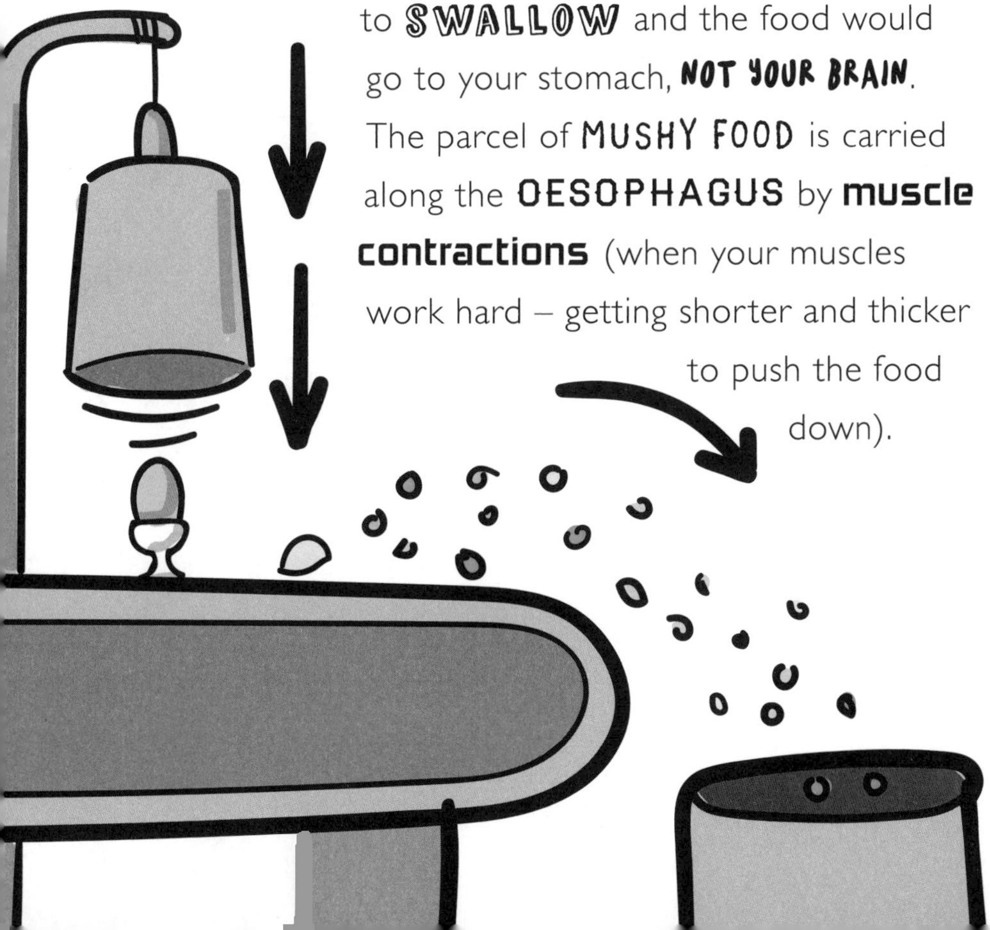

Even **astronauts** in **SPACE** can swallow **normally** and they have no idea which way's up or down.

Do you remember the acids we found attacking our teeth earlier? The stomach contains really strong acids too, but this time they are there to help us, by taking our food apart into **useful** stuff. After anything from **two to six hours**, your **STOMACH** then pushes everything out into the **small intestine** where it takes a trip on what looks, on a diagram, like the most **ROUND-ABOUTY, CRAZY** WATERSLIDE in the world...

WHHhhhheeeeeeeeeeeee

In a grown-up it's only about **30 cm (1 foot)** in a **straight line** from the **STOMACH** to the **BUM**, but the **intestines** don't go in a **straight** line. In fact, they are are **PACKED** so **TIGHTLY** inside this becomes a **7.5 metre (25 foot) journey** that takes about **40 HOURS**. As the food **TRAVELS** along, your body absorbs all the **LOVELY nutrients** from it into your blood.

But what is it your body is trying to **extract**? Well, there are **MANY THINGS** your food is made from and we use them for different jobs.

CARBOHYDRATES contain lots of energy that your body can use. They are found in things like **pasta**, **POTATOES**, **bread**, RICE and **sugary foods**. Often 'carbs' make a meal feel filling, and they make a great fuel, in the right amounts.

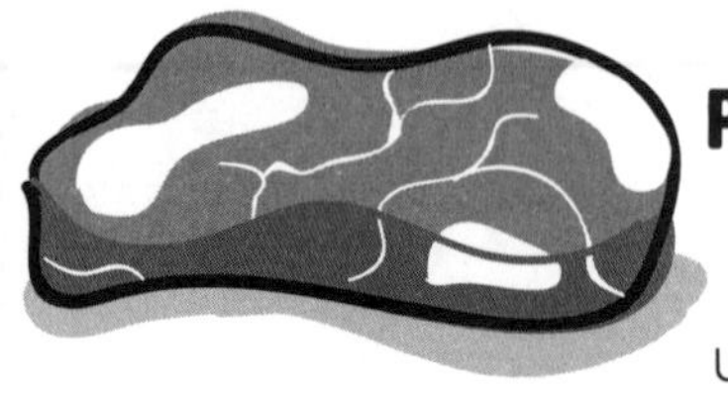

PROTEIN is found in **CHEESE**, **meat**, **FISH**, **beans**, and so on. Your body uses protein to help repair damaged tissue and make muscle, bone and skin. It also uses proteins to make some of the chemicals it needs to function, such as hormones and enzymes.

MICRONUTRIENTS are vitamins and minerals that your body needs in **small** amounts to **grow**

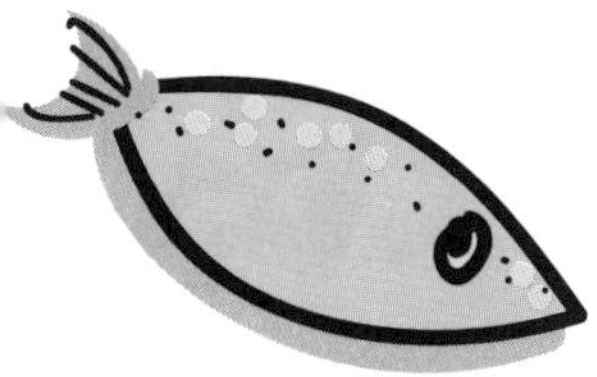

and produce hormones, enzymes and proteins, all madly **USEFUL THINGS.**

FATS are found in **meat**, **dairy**, **FISH**, **nuts** and **oils**. People are always worried about fats, but that's mainly when we eat too much of them. Your body, however, uses fat in loads of **USEFUL** ways: to keep your skin and tissues healthy, for example, as well as to transport

vitamins around the body. The human brain is nearly 60 per cent fat! Fat is also **essential** for your **nervous system** because we use it to make myelin, a substance that wraps around all of your **NERVE CELLS**, so they can **safely** send all those electrical messages. Fat is also used to make some **HORMONES**, those chemical messengers the body sends out to start and stop processes.

So, yes, **FAT** is handy stuff, but we can have too much of a good thing. **Just ask your dad's belly.**

What happens when we eat too much?

Everything your body **DOES** needs energy, which it gets from the food you **EAT**. *RUNNING*, JUMPING, **sitting**, **THINKING**, even **sleeping**, all use up **ENERGY**. Some activities use up **MORE** energy, like ***RACING*** up hills or **CARTWHEELING** down them, or whatever you like doing for **EXERCISE**, while others, like **reading**, **daydreaming**, watching television or **twiddling your thumbs**, use much **LESS**. Basically though, even when you're sitting still, you're still warm, so some fuel must be being burned inside you, **right?**

When you **EAT**, you take in **ENERGY** from your food. If all your *RUNNING*, **CARTWHEELING** and **sitting** doesn't use up all that energy, your body stores it for later, a bit like a **SQUIRREL** burying **nuts** for winter. Your body

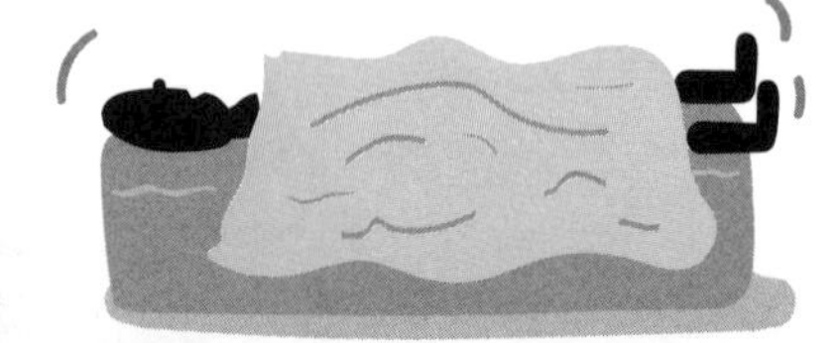

stores the energy by turning it into **FAT**, which it saves in handy spots to use later. This **CLEVER** system means you can go a while without eating, using the **ENERGY** in your fat cells until you eat again.

But how does your body burn fat? It's not like you have an oil or fat-burning stove tucked away. That would be **RIDICULOUS**. Instead, your body breathes it out through your lungs. **See?** That makes much more sense.

What? I just breathed out a pizza?

Well, **YES**, but in a really **COMPLICATED** way...

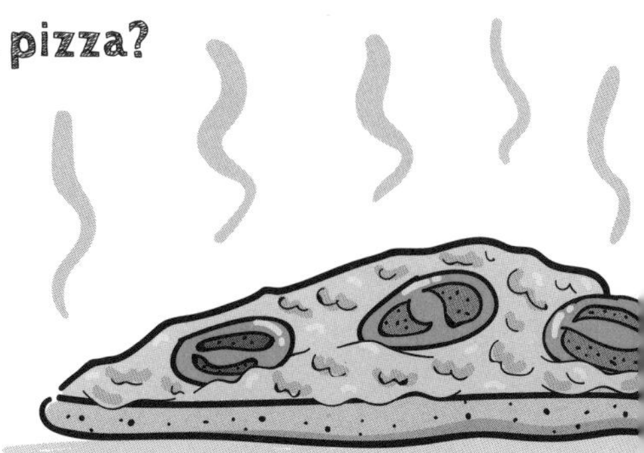

Like everything else, **FAT** is made of molecules, just really **complex ones**.

Water, which we mentioned earlier, is a really simple molecule with just one oxygen and two hydrogen atoms linked together. But fats are made up of loads of **hydrogen**, **carbon** and **oxygen** atoms all joined together in a **complicated** chain like this one:

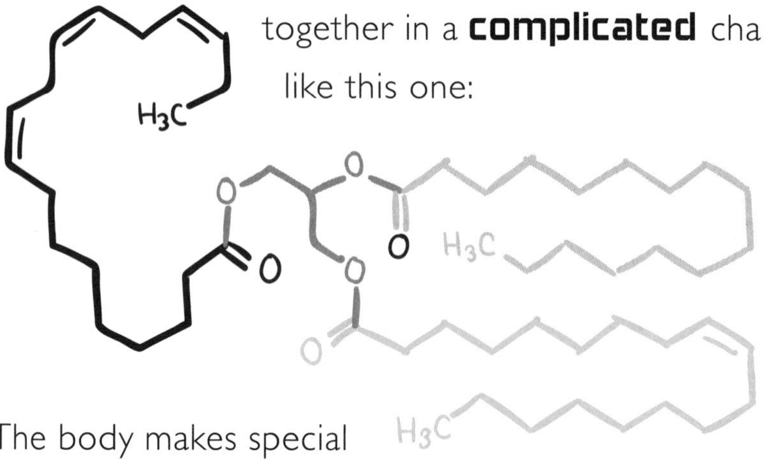

The body makes special chemicals called **'ENZYMES'**, which are really useful after you eat a meal because they are able to **BREAK DOWN** those **BIG FATTY** molecules you've eaten into smaller parts called 'fatty acids' and **'GLYCEROL'** – these are then released into your **BLOOD**. Your blood carries the fatty acids and glycerol around your body until they reach your liver, which transforms them into GLUCOSE (a sort of sugar) for your body to use as ENERGY. Your body 'BURNS' that fuel, by breaking the glucose down into **carbon dioxide** and **water**, which it breathes out with your lungs, while releasing heat and ENERGY.

This all happens in a lot of STAGES, as you can see, but the basic idea is SIMPLE: your body can take really **COMPLICATED** molecules **and break them down**, and find the parts of them that are **USEFUL** to burn for heat and energy, then breathe out the stuff that's left.

It's like if you had a heater at home that worked by burning **Lego pieces**, and you got really good at taking apart complete Lego models into the **individual pieces**, just to keep that heater going.

Has all this talk of **TRANSFORMING FAT MOLECULES** into **carbon dioxide** and water made you **HUNGRY?** Well, now you know why you eat **FOOD** and what your body does with it, it's time to decide what to have for **BREAKFAST...**

A toast to toast!

How about a slice of toast? I mean, it's just **HEATED BREAD**, isn't it? And yet... have you ever wondered why toast tastes so **DIFFERENT** to bread? Or why the **SMELL** of toast makes your mouth water? Or how a toaster transforms a piece of dull bread into a **CRUNCHY DELIGHT?**

To find this out, first let's have a look at your **TOASTER**. Toasters work using **electrical energy** that's produced by power stations and sent **WHIZZING** through wires to your home and, when you plug it in, out into your toaster. This electrical energy is similar to the electricity that had your hair standing on end ('static' electricity), but static electricity is called 'static' because it stays **still**. The electricity that produces the heat in your toaster is moving – it's an ***ELECTRICAL CURRENT*** (yep, that sounds like a river, and that's not a bad comparison to keep in mind with all those electrons flowing along).

Basically, a power station makes loads of spare electrons (remember them, from when they messed up your hair?) and, as we said before, they have a negative, or minus charge and they **DESPERATELY** want to find positives, or pluses they can hook up with. They are **SOOO** desperate to do this, we can send them down miles of electrical wires and do **LOADS OF WORK** for us, as they look for a **plus** to latch on to.

It's exactly the same as when you put a **battery** into, say, a **TOY CAR**. One side of the battery is minus (all the electrons) and the other side is plus (all the positive chemicals, missing an electron) and they are desperate to **GET TOGETHER**. So, all the electrons ***RACE*** out of the battery in a big loop, called a **'circuit'**, to get to the plus side, and while they are running their energy pushes the motor **ROUND AND ROUND** and **makes the car move**. **Or lights the headlights**. **Or makes a doll talk**. Or any sort of job we can think of.

Eventually enough **minuses** reach the **plus** side, and there is no longer a **HUGE** difference between one side of the battery and the other and it runs out of power and has to be **REPLACED**. Don't be **SAD** when you replace a battery. It isn't **DEAD**.

IT'S JUST HAPPY.

Happy to have finally **REUNITED** all the electrons with the chemicals they were taken from.

We're home!

So, in **FANCY** talk, electrical current is the **movement** of electrons through a material, such as the **wires of your toaster**. And to understand it more easily; just like the current of a *FAST-FLOWING* river, electrons stream through wires all the way from the power station to your **TOASTER.**

Take a look **INSIDE** your toaster once you've pushed down the lever. **WHAT DO YOU SEE?** Probably your bread, held between rows of **wires** that are glowing **BRIGHT RED**.

These **GLOWING RED** wires are called **'FILAMENTS'** and are very **THIN**. They are your toaster's **HEAT-PRODUCING SECRET**. As the electrons **WHIZZ** through the wires, they bump into one another and **COLLIDE** with the atoms that make up the metal wire. As they do this they give off **heat energy**.

If you and your friends were ***RUNNING*** through a crowded space you'd all be bumping off each other and releasing energy, usually by shouting, **"OW!"** and, **"GET OFF!"** The people who were already there, before you came running through, are now getting **BUMPED** and jostled and having their feet

STAMPED on and they are getting pretty hot and **ANGRY** about it.

We talked earlier about how atoms are arranged. In the middle are the heavy bits – the **PROTONS** and **NEUTRONS** – and then, orbiting them in a cloud, are the **ELECTRONS**. The middle is positive and the electrons are negative and all is balanced and **HAPPY**.

Then this mad stream of **LOOSE ELECTRONS** from the power station, or the battery, comes ***RACING*** past, full of energy and **SHOVING** and **BANGING** into things. They bump into the electrons who were already there, get them all **EXCITED** and full of energy and now the electrons have to do something with the energy. **SO THEY JUMP!** They go from the orbit they had, to one further out.

BUT THEY ARE NOT SUPPOSED TO BE THERE!

It's a bit like if someone gave you a **FIZZY** drink and the bubbles and the sugar and the thrill of it gave you a sudden **HUGE** burst of energy and you got all **EXCITED** and decided to go into a **CLASS** of kids five years older than you. And then you looked around and went, **"Whoa! I'm not supposed to be here."**

But the only way to go back to your classroom is to get rid of the **FIZZY GAS** from the drink, so you do a huge **BURP** and drop back to your classroom. Just like the electron getting rid of its extra energy and floating back down to its cloud.

BUUUUUURP

Excuse me?

Enjoy your breakfast!

So, electrons are just like you, really. They get all excited by this passing crowd, and **BOUNCED** into a really big orbit, way further out than they should be, so they **BURP** out the extra energy as **LIGHT** and **HEAT** and that's what you see and feel from the toaster filaments.

Lots of things in your house produce **HEAT** in this way, your **kettle**, the grill in your cooker, and even your **WASHING MACHINE** all turn electrical energy into heat energy by passing it through a NARROW WIRE.

So, to sum up, electrons are **RUDE**, and they **PUSH** and **SHOVE** and get other electrons **EXCITED**, and the other electrons **BURP** until your toast is brown.

Which all makes perfect sense. **But why does it taste so yummy?** Well that's because of **DUCKS**, of course.

The Maillard reaction

POP! Your toast is done. Doesn't it look delicious? But what is it about toast that makes it so much yummier than bread? **What happens to it in the toaster?**

The **MALLARD REACTION** is what happens. Ducks **LOVE** bread, and **HATE** toast. So, if you give toast to a mallard (a type of duck) it'll quack **ANGRILY** and that's when you know the toast is done.

No, wait. I've misread that. **Mallard – that's a DUCK.** The **Maillard** reaction is named after **Louis-Camille Maillard**, a chemist from France, who was the first person to describe this **DELICIOUS TOASTING PROCESS.**

MALLARD

BREAD is made of **flour**, and **flour** includes **CARBOHYDRATES** and **PROTEINS**. When you pop your slice of bread in the toaster and press down the lever, **HEAT** from the toaster causes the sugars and chemicals in the proteins called '**AMINO ACIDS**', to **COMBINE**, and that creates the caramel colour and the **YUMMY** smell.

The heat also makes some of the **WATER** in the surface of your bread **EVAPORATE**, drying it out and making it nice and **CRUNCHY**.

So, **nothing** to do with **DUCKS** at all then. But well done **Louis-Camille Maillard**, the scientist who worked on toast.

So, why does it make your mouth water?

When we **SMELL** food, we anticipate eating it, so the body starts the machinery running **in advance**. The first stage of this is **SALIVA IN THE MOUTH**, ready to break down the food, ready for the yummy **tasting** to happen...

Tongue-tastic!

How does that breakfast taste? Is it SWEET? **Salty?** How about **UMAMI?**

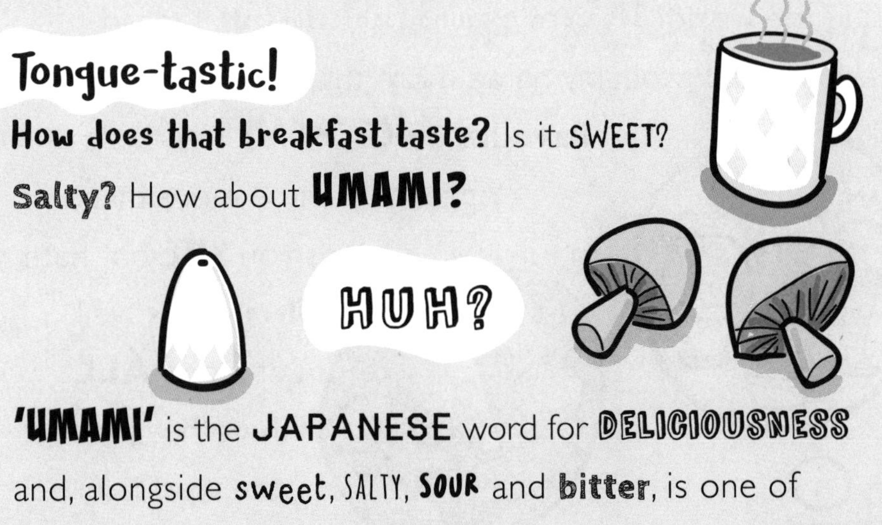

'UMAMI' is the **JAPANESE** word for **DELICIOUSNESS** and, alongside **sweet**, SALTY, **SOUR** and **bitter**, is one of the five tastes that make up all of our foods.

SWEET is the taste of **sugar**; SALT, well, that one is obvious. **UMAMI** is the smoky taste of **COOKED MEAT** or **MUSHROOMS**; and even though they are used to describe similar things, **SOUR** is how a **LEMON** tastes and **bitter** is more like **coffee**. That seems like **TWO NICE** ones and **THREE HORRIBLE** ones to me, which is pretty unfair.

Just five basic tastes to make up **ALL** the tastes in the world? It doesn't sound right, does it? I mean you could probably name more than **five different flavours** of **ICE CREAM**. You could probably name more than five foods you **HATE**, but hate **differently**, as well. Let alone **ALL** the other foods in the world.

Well, there may be more to it than just **TASTE**.

Many scientists now want to add **'starchiness'** and **'fatty'** to the list of flavours that your tongue can detect and some think that other tastes, such as **'calcium'**, **'amino acids'** and even the **not-so-yummy-sounding** **'BLOOD'** may also need to be added to the list.

Your body detects all these things with your **TONGUE**. Your tongue is covered with **taste receptors**, which pick up on all of the five **(and maybe more)** tastes and send **MESSAGES** via your nervous system to your brain to tell you whether you are tasting sweet, SALTY, **UMAMI TOAST** or **bitter**, sweet lemonade and so on.

Your tongue has **touch receptors** as well as taste receptors. These touch receptors tell you how **WARM**, **SPICY**, **ROUGH**, **smooth** or **CREAMY**

the food is and so play a big part in letting you know how the food **TASTES**.

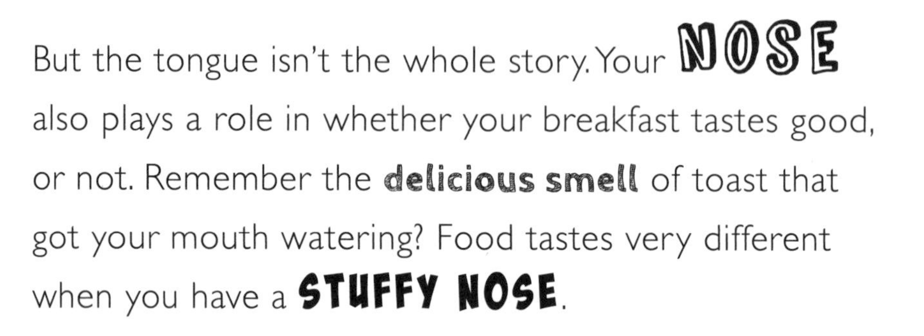

But the tongue isn't the whole story. Your **NOSE** also plays a role in whether your breakfast tastes good, or not. Remember the **delicious smell** of toast that got your mouth watering? Food tastes very different when you have a **STUFFY NOSE**.

Let's find out why. Here's the greatest experiment in all of science.

Take a piece of **CHOCOLATE**. Before you pop it in your mouth – **wait, have you already put it in your mouth?**

Okay, have a mouthful of water and we'll start again. Take a piece of chocolate. **DON'T** put it in your mouth. **You've put it your mouth again, haven't you?**

Come on! Right. More water.

Take a piece
of chocolate. **DON'T!**
Good. Now, before you put it in your mouth, **hold your nose closed** with your other hand so you **can't** breathe through it. **NOW** put the **CHOCOLATE** in your mouth. **Let it melt**. It's pretty nice, right? While it's **melting** on your tongue, though, take your fingers off your nose and breathe through it. **WHOOSH!** It suddenly tastes

AMAZING!

That's because, while you have **taste receptors** on your tongue, you sense **FLAVOURS** in your **NOSE**.

We say the words **'TASTE'** and **'FLAVOUR'** as if they are the same thing, but what we are talking about is usually a **mixture** of the **two**: taste on the tongue, flavour in the nose.

And here's the important part: if that didn't work for you... **Get more chocolate and try it again, and again until it does.**

It's what a scientist would do.

STOP EATING CHOCOLATE FOR BREAKFAST!

All right, let's **SCRAMBLE** some **EGGS** in the microwave instead.

The Superhero Magnetron

Crack some **EGGS** into a bowl, give them a **WHISK** with a fork, and then pop them onto the turntable and wait until: **PING!** A delicious pile of steaming **SCRAMBLED EGGS**. **Piping hot**.

But how does the microwave heat them up?

HA! That's easy, says your mum or dad. There is PROBABLY a heating element somewhere inside, just like your toaster or kettle or grill.

Nope, *you say.* There's **no** heating element. Instead, microwaves have something called a **MAGNETRON**. Which sounds like the name of some kind of very cool **SUPERHERO**.

Or a **ROBOT** that turns into a truck. But it isn't. It's **waaaay** cooler than that.

We keep mentioning the amazing **INVISIBLE** things all around you, and here's one of the **MOST AMAZING**. Something called **'ELECTROMAGNETIC WAVES'**, which is a big fancy name, but they're pretty **important** since they are both invisible, and also **every single thing you see**.

Hmmm. This may be hard to explain, so let's take a **DEEP BREATH.**

We've mentioned already about how all the matter in the **UNIVERSE** is made up of **protons** and **neutrons** and **electrons**, and how protons have a positive charge and electrons have a negative charge. So, **EVERYWHERE** around us are these electric charges jostling around at the TINIEST level, in what are called 'electromagnetic fields'.

If you bring a **MAGNET** **slowly** nearer another **MAGNET**, you can feel the **PUSH** or **PULL** as you get closer. That's the **MAGNETIC FIELD** changing right there. It's pretty obvious because it gets so **STRONG** as they get really close; but we walk through a universe that is **AT EVERY POINT** feeling the **PUSH** and **PULL** of all the electrical charges and magnetic forces around us. We don't feel it except when it gets really **STRONG**, but it's **always** there, **EVERYWHERE** around us.

We walk through this **ELECTROMAGNETIC FIELD** a bit like how a **fish swims through the sea**; we don't even know it's there. And similarly to how in the sea you can have **WAVES** in water and the **fish** carries on regardless, there are waves in this electrical 'sea', **ALL AROUND US**, at all times.

These are called **ELECTROMAGNETIC WAVES** and they do some pretty **AMAZING** things. For one thing, a simpler name for some of them would be **'LIGHT'**.

Yep, all light is just a type of wave, a regular up-and-down wobble, passing through the electromagnetic field all around us.

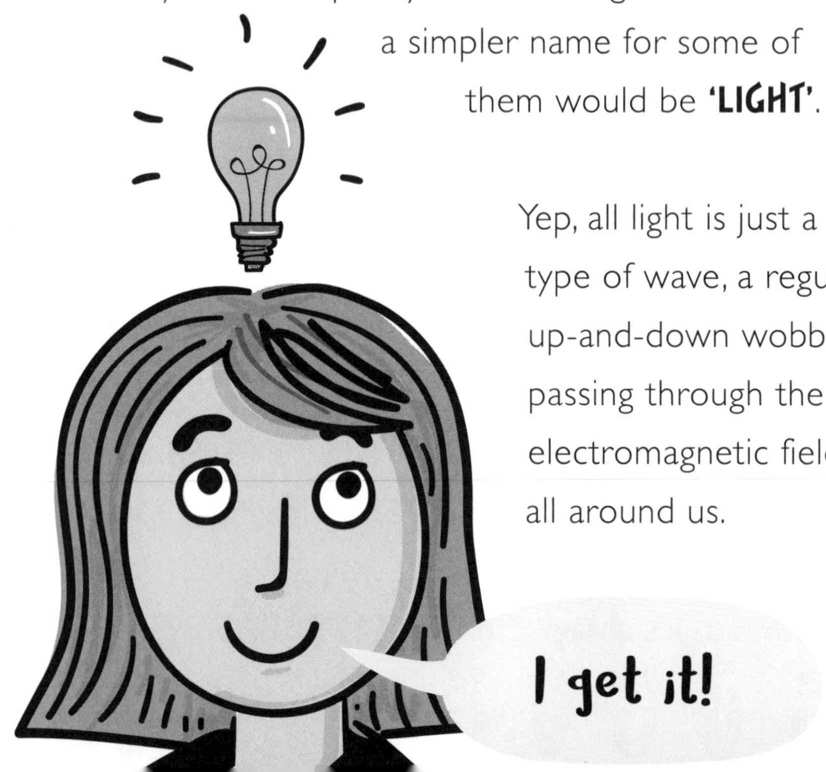

Some **WAVES** are **LONG** and **DEEP**; and some are **short** and **punchy**.

And the different **SHAPES** behave quite differently, mainly because they carry different amounts of **ENERGY**.

The **LONG** and **DEEP** waves we call '**RADIO WAVES**', and yes, that's what **radios** can **RECEIVE**, and the **computer** on **wifi** and **radio telescopes** staring into space. They are all machines built to pick up **LONG**, **DEEP WAVES**. As the waves get **shorter**, the peaks come more often, and as the peaks come more often they carry more **ENERGY**, and more information. After **RADIO WAVES**, there are **MICROWAVES**. This is what mobile phones use to communicate.

So, we can send out our own **wobbles** in the **ELECTROMAGNETIC FIELD** to talk to people.

And then there's the waves in a TINY section that are not **too long**, and not **too short**, which our eyes have become **really good** at recognizing as **VISIBLE LIGHT**. So, all the colours of the spectrum are different types of **ELECTROMAGNETIC WAVES**, and our eyes and brains are built to see them as the **COLOURS** of the world around us. We **can't** see **RADIO WAVES** though, although we know they are there.

And then there are the **really short** waves that come at you **Bump! Bump! BUMP!** really fast. These are the waves with the **MOST ENERGY**, with fabulous names like **'GAMMA RAYS'** and **'X-RAYS'**. They are so **POWERFUL** they can travel right through you and we can use them take **pictures** of your **INSIDES**, but they are also very **DANGEROUS** because of the amount of **ENERGY** they carry.

WHOA! We were talking about **MICROWAVES!** Now I remember why this all started.

Yes, you wanted some **scrambled eggs**, right? And we ended up all over the **UNIVERSE**.

Microwaves are like a type of light, except they have **LOADS** of energy and they can pass **through** things. So, where does the magnetron come into it? Well, it takes the electricity from the plug and turns it into these microwaves, which are like radio waves, but much **smaller** and more **POWERFUL**.

Once the **MICROWAVES** meet the food, they make the molecules inside it **vibrate** very fast. As we know from the element in the toaster, when **atoms** and **molecules vibrate** and bump against each other they **HEAT UP**, cooking your **YUMMY EGGS** or whatever else you decide to cook in there.

Phew! Still with us? **Have an egg!** And **FOOL** your parents!

Yummy lovely eggs! But where did they come from?

Yes, the fridge. **But before that?**

Yes, the shop. You're doing this deliberately, aren't you?

Where do eggs ORIGINALLY come from?

Chickens, of course!

But where did the chicken come from? That's right! **AN EGG!** And that came from a **chicken** before that, which was an **EGG** before that, which came from a **chicken** before that, and **so on**.

So, ask your mum or dad, or teacher, which came first, the **chicken** or the **EGG?**

They'll probably **HUFF** and **PUFF** and say that there's **NO ANSWER**, because people have been struggling with the question all the way back to the ancient Greeks, **BUT**... actually, **THERE** is an answer.

The ancient **GREEKS** were great with, but didn't know anything about, **DINOSAURS**. We have found fossils of eggs, however, dated to around **190 million years ago**, right bang in the age of the dinosaurs.

We don't think there were any **chickens** around back then. In fact, the earliest bird-like fossil is the Archaeopteryx and it dates from **150 million years ago**.

So, eggs were around a long time before chickens even arrived.

And while your **mum** or **dad** looks confused by that...

Steal their toast.
And eggs.
And cereal.
You need the energy – you have lots more to do today!

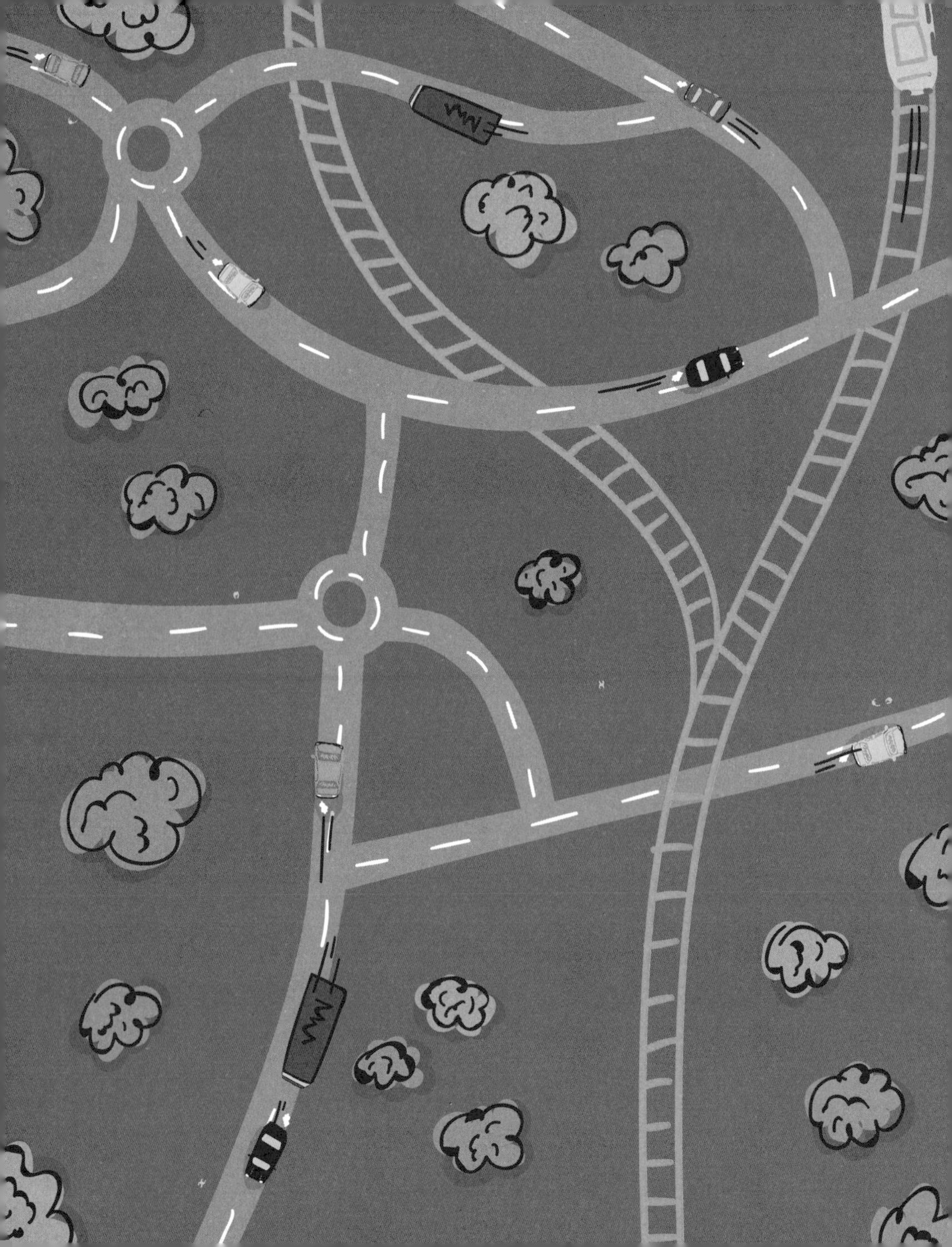

Let's Get
On-board the
Exploding Fish!

You've **EATEN** your **BREAKFAST** so you've got some **fuel** in your engine. **Time to get moving!**

The chances are that today is just one of those **ORDINARY** days where you're making the **SAME** journey you always do – *DRAGGING* yourself to school.

Or being dragged...

Being pulled along the road is probably the most **EFFICIENT**, **energy-saving** way of getting to school. For **you**, that is; **not** for your mum or dad. I mean, you could just stay wrapped in a duvet and still get pulled all the way to school. Or you could make it even **EASIER** for your mum and dad...

But let's presume you're one of those people who **doesn't**

get dragged all the way to school. Let's say you **WALK**, or **CYCLE** or – **lucky you!** – **GET DRIVEN** all the way there.

Which one is the most efficient?

We compare **'EFFICIENCY'** in how much energy it takes to do the **same** job. If you had to **tidy your room** and could either do it normally, or do it while you could only **hop from bed to rug to bed**, because, of course, the carpet is made of **LAVA**, well, one of those methods is much **LESS 'EFFICIENT'** than the other. You get the same result, but use **LOADS** more energy. This is why scientists always say, **don't build your bedroom on lava.**

One of the ways we measure energy is by using **CALORIES**, by the way, which you've probably heard of with regard to food. It's basically a measure of how much **ENERGY (mainly heat)** is released when something is burned. Food scientists actually find out how many calories something has by setting **FIRE** to it and measuring how **HOT** it gets. That is literally somebody's job, **TO SET FIRE TO FOOD.**

So, which is the most efficient and the best use of your energy on your morning commute?

Well, **WALKING ISN'T**, for a start. **CYCLING** is **waaaayyy** more **EFFICIENT** than walking. **How much more?** Amazingly, it's a about **FIVE TIMES** more **EFFICIENT**, which means that for the same amount of **energy** you spend in walking to school, you could cycle there, realize that you'd **FORGOTTEN** your pencil, **cycle home**, grab the pencil, **cycle back** to school, realize you'd forgotten your gym kit, **cycle home**, grab it and then **cycle back** to school again. See how much more **EFFICIENT** that journey is?

Now, who forgot to bring in their lunch?

Oh, no...

You can compare **CYCLING** to walking and running just by watching how our **LEGS move**. When we **RUN** or **WALK**, we move by using our legs to push down on the ground and propel us forward. So much of the **energy** we use is wasted by **SLAMMING** our feet into the floor and **lifting** our bodies up again. When you cycle though, that downward push is changed by the **pedals** and **gears** into SPINNING the back wheel, so most of the energy goes into moving us *FORWARD*.

Plus, if you're **WALKING** or **RUNNING** and you stop moving your legs, you **STOP** moving. On a bike, even UPHILL you'll carry on moving a bit, because the wheels store the **energy** for a little while even when you're not pedalling to add more energy. **Enjoy freewheeling, it's all your energy!**

Time to freewheel... Oh...

Plus, cycling is *FASTER*. So, if you were in something faster again, say, **A CAR**, would that be even more **EFFICIENT?**

Oh no. No, no, no. Cars are **TERRIBLY** inefficient, at least next to bikes.

ONE HUNDRED KILOCALORIES OF FUEL in a **CYCLIST** might keep them going for 4 and a half kms (3 miles) depending on how fit they are. With the same amount of fuel, the average petrol or diesel-powered car can travel less than **100 metres!**

Cars are **INEFFICIENT** partly because they are so **HEAVY**. That big metal frame, the glass and steel, all those comics and magazines on the floor and at least two people (unless you were planning on driving yourself).

When you **CYCLE**, your body unlocks the chemical **energy** from the food you eat and uses it to make the **MUSCLES** in your legs *PUSH* **down** on the pedals, which turns the wheels on your bicycle, turning it into **kinetic energy**, which is the energy of something moving. That all sounds very **TIRING**. But nothing like the efforts to make a car move.

When you travel in a car, the engine unlocks:

1. the **chemical energy** in the fuel.

2. the **electrical energy** from the car's battery.

The car uses these two things to make **movement energy** and it all happens in the **ENGINE**.

Inside a car's **engine**, small amounts of fuel and compressed air are held in a closed chamber called a **'cylinder'**. Sparks from the spark plugs **IGNITE** the petrol and it **EXPLODES**. The energy of this little explosion pushes levers inside the engine called **'pistons'**. Pistons are a bit like the pedals of your bike, as they turn the **gears** and, with explosion after explosion, the wheels beneath the car begin to turn. Then it **TRANSPORTS** you all the way to the school gate; or at least to the end of the next **queue of traffic**, or **traffic light**, or **zebra crossing**, or **lollipop lady**.

So, it all seems quite different to the **energy** you use to ride a bike, except for one important **similarity**. The energy in PETROL comes originally from the same place as the energy in your FOOD, and that place, **SURPRISINGLY**, is **150 MILLION KILOMETRES**

(93 million miles) away.

All our energy comes from...

THE SUN.

Yep, ultimately, the car and the cyclist are both **SOLAR-POWERED**, and so is just about **everything** else on Earth.

But quite A LOT has to **happen** to the solar energy from the Sun before it starts **pedalling you to school**.

SUNLIGHT

is used by plants
to make their food.
Plants do this with an
AMAZING process called
'PHOTOSYNTHESIS'. Do you
remember how, in the last chapter,
we broke down complex **food molecules** to
find **fuel** to burn and then released heat and
breathed out the gases? Photosynthesis is
a little like the **OPPOSITE** of that.
The plants use light from the Sun
to transform carbon dioxide
(from the air around them)
and water (which they take in
through their roots)
into sugars.

ANIMALS –
let's say **people** –
eat these plants, or
the animals that have
eaten the plants (let's say
cows or **chickens**), and get the
energy from the **SUGARS** inside and use
it to **POWER** them through their day.

So, where does petrol come into this? Do petrol stations eat vegetables (or chickens)?

Petrol comes from **CRUDE**, or unrefined, **OIL**. Oil comes from deep **below** the ground and is mainly formed from the remains of tiny plants and animals that lived in the world's oceans **MANY MILLIONS OF YEARS AGO**.

When these TINY PLANTS and **animals**, and probably a fair few **FISH**, died, they sank to the bottom of the oceans and **PILED UP**. As they lay there they became buried beneath **SAND** and **SEDIMENT**. As the sand or sediment built up over these **DEAD** plants and fish, they began to break down or **DECAY**. But this decay was a little different to how plants and animals are usually allowed to decay. Just look in a fruit bowl and you'll see how plants decay. They go brown and smell and then you throw them out. **This was different though**.

The sediment and the seawater on top of them, **BLOCKED** out any air, which would usually help release the energy held in their bodies.

In other words, the plants and animals were closed off from the air, so they couldn't decay. This means the energy in their bodies was trapped.

And the **BRILLIANT** thing about energy is that it can't just **DISAPPEAR**. It's a scientific law. The First Law of **Thermodynamics**, in fact:

"Energy cannot be created or destroyed in a closed system."

And there are few systems quite as closed as this. **CRUSHED** between layers of **sedimentary rock** (rock formed of fine sand and particles) **beneath the ocean**, with **NO AIR** to help them rot properly. That's about as **ISOLATED** as it gets, so the **energy** locked up in the bodies of these plants and animals stayed right there.

The lack of air and the immense **FORCE**, or **PRESSURE**, of the weight of the sediment as well as **HEAT** from inside the Earth transforms these dead plants and animals (and the energy locked up inside them) into a substance called **'KEROGEN'**, which eventually turns into **OIL** and **GAS**, which we extract from the ground, and process into something easy to **BURN**, like petrol. Then we can **PUMP IT** into our cars and get moving!

When the person **DRIVING** the car turns on the ignition and you hear the engine **ROARING** into life, you are hearing thousands of MINIATURE **EXPLOSIONS** created from the **ENERGY** those tiny plants and animals captured from sunlight **MANY MILLIONS OF YEARS AGO**.

So, you can see that you using the **energy** from your **BREAKFAST** to **cycle** to school is a bit more **efficient** than waiting **MILLIONS OF YEARS** for dead algae and plankton to turn into PETROL.

Here's a question, though: **would a car be more efficient if it could carry more people?**

Maybe with two levels of seats for **LOADS** of passengers and a **regular route** so people knew where it was going to STOP and... **oh wait**, I've just invented the **BUS**, haven't I?

But why do buses travel in threes?

Buses are **GREAT**. They transport **large numbers** of people cheaply and they **SAVE** having a load more cars on the road. The problem with buses is the **WAITING AROUND**. And the **OTHER PROBLEM** with buses is STRANGE PEOPLE also waiting for buses turning to you out of the blue and saying:

"The thing about buses, you wait forever for one bus and then two come along at once."

And you **nod**, and **roll your eyes**, and quietly move away from the strange person. **But wait!** The strange person is **RIGHT**. Buses do come in **TWOS!** And sometimes **THREES!** There's a even a name for this. It's called the **'CLUMPING EFFECT'**.

In fact, there are at least three other names for it as well: **'bus bunching'**, **'convoying'** and **'platooning'**. People waiting for buses have a lot of time to think about **names** for things.

So, what is the truth behind this, or is it just that **bus drivers** like to be **CLOSE** to other **bus drivers** so they can **CHAT IN TRAFFIC?**

When buses set off in the morning, they leave **one at a time**, at their regularly **SPACED** intervals and, in an ideal world, this is how they would stay. **BUT**, as you know, **things don't always go to plan**. Life gets in the way. Lots of life. There's **TRAFFIC** and **PEDESTRIANS** and **FAMILIES OF DUCKS** crossing the road to get to another pond, all **the usual stuff**.

Once a bus is **DELAYED**, it means there's more time for people to gather at stops further down the route. The **more people** there are at each stop the **LONGER** they take to get on the bus. In fact, the

number one reason for buses being late **isn't ducks**. The number one reason is: people getting ON AND OFF buses.

When **bus number two** gets to the stop, there are fewer people waiting to board because half of them UNEXPECTEDLY got on the **first bus**. This means **bus number two** doesn't have to wait so long at the stop as it would usually, so it can pull away QUICKER and make up EVEN MORE TIME on **bus number one**.

As this happens **over** and **over AGAIN**, it doesn't take long until **bus number two** is RIGHT BEHIND **bus number one**. It might even OVERTAKE **bus one** and then it gets **slowed down** as well. Before long

you might even have a **bus number three** involved, which not even the STRANGE PERSON saw coming.

There is a solution for this, but it's an **UNPOPULAR** one. Simply **LIMIT** the amount of **TIME** the buses are allowed to **STOP** at each stop, then **close the doors** and drive off. Yeah, I can see how that would be **UNPOPULAR.**

It would be **NECESSARY** though, if you had the kind of buses that **COULDN'T overtake each other.** That would be the sort of bus that might run on TRACKS, say. **Oh wait**, I've just invented **THE TRAIN**.

Trains don't care about you

For trains, **CLUMPING** is a much **BIGGER** problem because they **CAN'T OVERTAKE** each other, so you would be left with one full, SLOW train, followed by one or two **EMPTY** trains.

So, trains are much **stricter** about sticking to a timetable. They'll leave, even if there are people left on the platform. On the London Underground there is an **alarm** to say the doors are about to **CLOSE**. In Tokyo, in order to get people on the train quickly during rush hour, there are special staff called **'oshiya'**, or **'pushers'**, who **SHOVE** people on board the train to squash them all in.

Still, once you're on the train you can **RELAX** and listen to the **CALMING CLICKETY CLACK** of the tracks. **What do you mean you can't hear that?** Oh yeah, trains **DON'T** often sound like that **ANY MORE**.

All trains used to make that noise because the tracks had **GAPS** in them, called **'EXPANSION GAPS'**. The gaps were there because train tracks are made of **steel** and **carbon.** As the tracks heated up, the atoms in the steel and carbon had more **ENERGY** and wanted to move about more, which made the tracks **EXPAND**. So, the expansion gaps gave tracks room to stretch when they were warm.

ULTIMATELY, give them enough **energy** and the atoms would **PUSH** away from each other completely and **MELT** the tracks, but that would have to be a **very**, **very HOT DAY**, when the temperature reached over **1,300°C**, which is **HOTTER** than the

HOTTEST planet in the **Solar System**, so we should be fine.

What's the big deal?

This all might not **seem** like a big deal, and it wouldn't be if there was just a little bit of track. But there isn't, there are **MILES** of track, which makes it a **HUGE DEAL** for the railways that still use these older clickety-clack trains. Too much **EXPANSION** would make the track **bend** and **buckle**, **tearing** the bolts right out of the sleepers, leaving your train with **NOWHERE TO GO**.

The **EXPANSION GAPS** give the steel track room to **stretch** out in the **warm** sun without rendering

the whole rail network **USELESS**. So, pretty important. Remember that the next time you hear:

**CLICK-ET-Y CLACK, CLICK-ET-Y CLACK,
EX-PAN-SION GAP, EX-PAN-SION GAP**

But as we said this sound is becoming a thing of the **PAST**. We want to get places *FASTER* and **HIGH-SPEED TRAINS** can't run on tracks with lots of gaps in it, so they need track that is welded together **SMOOTHLY**.

"But what about expansion?" you cry. "I've only just heard about it and now I'm frantic with worry that on a hot day the tracks will expand and warp and bend and melt and it will be a right old mess!"

Well, here comes the clever part. When the steel rails are made they are **stretched**. This

gives the iron and carbon atoms a little more **room** to **move around**. The tracks are laid under tension, which means they are **PULLED TIGHT**.

When the Sun **SHINES** on the tracks and they **HEAT UP**, the atoms move around and reach what is known as their **stress-free temperature**, but occupy the same space. It's like they relax into the space they have, like you climbing into a **DOUBLE BED** and **stretching** all your limbs out under the duvet.

But what happens when it gets **really**, **really HOT?** Well, when it gets really, really hot, the atoms in the steel rail will start to move around too much and yes, there is a danger that the rail will **BEND**.

Somebody has been thinking about this though, and worked out that to get these new **FANCY** *HIGH-SPEED RAILS* to get close to **buckling**, the temperature would have to be over **40°C**, a temperature that has **NEVER** been recorded in the United Kingdom. **Phew!**

So, sit back and enjoy your **SMOOTH**, **quiet**, **NON-CLUMPING** ride on a *SUPERFAST TRAIN*. You can even say the **clickety-clack** sound yourself, if you are feeling nostalgic.

So, where are we going anyway?

What, **school?** Who wants to learn **ANYTHING** about **SCHOOL?**

An Entire Chapter About School

Oh please. I wouldn't do that to you. Let's skip all that instead and do something more fun.

The Things You
Actually Want
to Do

Well, I'm glad that's **OVER WITH**, for today at least.

Teachers **NAGGING** you, **homework** needing to be delivered, **TESTS** being taken. Even in **PE**, which was a pain anyway because you forgot your kit, and then the ball came to you and you had chance to score but **SUDDENLY** everyone was **LOOKING AT YOU** and running towards you and your **brain was racing** and your **heart rate was up**...

All day long! Even when you get home, your **PARENTS** are all...

"So! What happened at school?"

"How was the test?"

"Did you remember your PE kit?"

"GET YOUR HOMEWORK DONE!"

"Practise your piano!"

You're just trying to **RELAX**, but you can't because they're **NAGGING** at you about stuff and it's getting your **heart rate up** and your **brain is racing** and... **wait a minute!** Why are your brain and your heart getting so INVOLVED in all this? **What's going on in there?**

What is happening in that brain of yours?

It's probably **STRESS**. You may have heard grown-ups talking about stress, but kids can feel stressed too.

Stress is your mind and body's response to **MENTAL** and **EMOTIONAL** tension. It's what you feel when you have lots to do and you aren't sure how it's going to get done; or when you have a **PROBLEM** you don't know how to fix; or when you are pretty sure there is a **SABRE-TOOTHED TIGER** outside your cave and you know you **have** to do something about it. And that last one is a good example of why stress **isn't always a bad thing.**

Stress is yet another part of the **INVISIBLE** world going on **INSIDE** your body helping you do what you need to do to survive. Without stress, human beings would have **DIED OUT** long ago, having been **eaten** by **PREDATORS** we didn't feel the need to run away from.

Instead, we (and other animals) developed a **chemical response** to **THREATENING** situations called **'FIGHT OR FLIGHT'**. Basically, the body can focus all its attention on sorting out the **BIGGEST** and most IMMEDIATE problem it has, which is, do I **FIGHT** this sabre-toothed tiger to survive, or do I **RUN AWAY?**

When your body is under stress, it releases chemical messengers called hormones to help you out. The main stress hormones are adrenaline and cortisol and, in the right circumstances, they can be your **BEST FRIENDS**.

Friends in a crisis

You've probably heard of **ADRENALINE**, as professional sports people talk about it all the time.

It's made in the **ADRENAL GLANDS**, which sit above your kidneys, right in your **middle**.

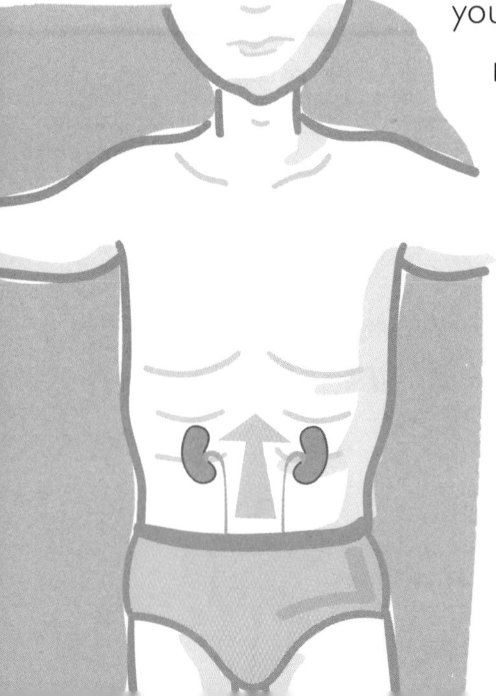

Adrenaline **INCREASES** your heart rate, which means blood moves around your body *FASTER*, giving your muscles everything they need, such as **oxygen** and **energy**,

to run (or fight, if it's a really TINY sabre-toothed tiger).

Cortisol is not as well-known. You rarely hear professional sports people talk about it, but it's pretty **USEFUL** nonetheless.

Cortisol increases the amount of **sugar** in your blood, which your body uses for energy. It also helps your body decide what functions are **IMPORTANT** in an **EMERGENCY STRESS** situation, and suppresses the ones that are less important. For example, systems such as your **digestive** and **immune system** (your body's defence against disease) are **hugely** important most of the time, but don't do much to help you **run from a sabre-toothed tiger** or **get you through a test**. So they can take a break while this is happening.

These stress **HORMONES** are great when they are coursing through your body, **HELPING** you get stuff done, making you think *QUICKLY*, helping your body move *FASTER* and react.

However, once the **THREAT** passes, it can be difficult for your body to get the word out to these **HORMONES** to stop doing what they do, and that can cause **PROBLEMS**.

Cortisol, for example, **OVERPOWERS** your immune system because that's not the priority during that sabre-toothed tiger **ATTACK**. However, the effect can last long after the danger has passed, which explains why **STRESS** can make you more likely to catch a **cold** or the **flu**.

After a **STRESSFUL DAY**, your body might be filled with

these stress hormones and it is **IMPORTANT** to take time to do something that will help you **RELAX**. Just tell your parents that this is **science** – you **need** to do it.

AND RELAX...

So, what will it be? How about curling up on the couch with your **DOG** or **CAT?** Lots of people find hanging out with animals **very relaxing** and, of course, the reason for this is: more hormones!

But **not** the hormones that stress you out – different hormones that can **CALM YOU DOWN** and help you to **RELAX**.

When you sit **stroking** your **FAVOURITE PET**, or even give your favourite person a big hug, your body releases a hormone called **'oxytocin'**. Oxytocin is a **lovely hormone**,

released by the pituitary gland in your **BRAIN** (it's the size of a pea and behind your nose). It is sometimes called the **'love chemical'** or **'cuddle chemical'** because of its **CALMING** effect on the body.

Oxytocin is also **BRILLIANT** because the more you have the more you get! This is called a **'POSITIVE FEEDBACK MECHANISM'** and it works like this:

Stroke your dog – your pituitary gland produces oxytocin making you feel **WARM** and **CALM** – which makes you stroke your dog some **more** – which makes your body produce **more** oxytocin – which makes you feel **WARM** and **CALM** – which makes you

STROKE YOUR DOG.

So, while the hormone **ADRENALINE** makes you want to **GET AWAY** from the thing that causes **STRESS**, and therefore get rid of the need for more adrenaline...

Oxytocin is fine **riiiight here**, making more lovely, lovely oxytocin.

But if you don't have a pet, or if you have a pet that cannot be petted, like a **GOLDFISH – do not pet the goldfish!** – what can you do to relax?

How about listening to your **favourite music?** What better way to **CALM** you down after a busy day? Music is a great **stress reliever**. Scientists have discovered that, like stroking your pet, music can help release **FEEL-GOOD** hormones, such as **oxytocin** and

a **neurotransmitter** (big word — will explain) called **dopamine** (okay, another big word — will now explain).

We've spoken about **HORMONES** a few times in this book, remember **ghrelin** to stop you eating, or **melatonin** to stop you sleeping? Maybe not, but I guarantee you'll recall how **ADRENALINE** will get you away from the **BIG SCARY SABRE-TOOTHED TIGER.**

Hormones are produced by **LITTLE FACTORIES** in your body called **'glands'** and are: **TRANSPORTED** around the body in your **BLOOD**.

'Neurotransmitters' are another type of chemical messenger in the body. This time though the chemical is produced by nerve cells called **NEURONS**, and the message can be carried via the nervous system, which is a bit like **telephone cabling** in your body that allows your brain to communicate with all the different parts of you.

It's reward time!

Dopamine is usually released when the body receives **REWARDS** that are valuable to it, such as **FOOD**, **MONEY** or **SLEEP**.

A study has shown that people respond to music in a similar way, that the mere **ANTICIPATION** of a favourite **BIT of a song** causes an increase in dopamine, in the same way as when you experience **PLEASURE** before taking a **BITE** of your **FAVOURITE FOOD**. Your body knows something good is going to happen to it and

rewards you with a hearty dose of **dopamine** – the feel-good chemical.

Interestingly, **more** dopamine is released when the reward is **UNEXPECTED**, which is why it is more **EXCITING** to hear your **FAVOURITE** song being **SUDDENLY** played on the radio, than when you choose it; and the **FIRST BITE** of the meal is more exciting than the next, and so on. One industry is **very good** at keeping that dopamine coming, and we'll get to that when we plug into a **CONSOLE** a little later...

It's all good. Until it isn't...

This is working out **GREAT!** You're stroking the **CAT**, or the **DOG** – **do not STROKE the goldfish, I cannot stress that enough** – and your favourite song is playing. You're a happy mix of **oxytocin** and tiny **dopamine** hits... and yet... something is **NIGGLING** at the back of your mind...

YOU HAVE STUFF TO DO.

Thoughts begin to **CREEP** into your mind ... **HOMEWORK** ... it needs to get done ... maybe later ... **one more song?... No!** Best get it done ... you know you'll feel **BETTER** when you get it done...

And there you are, listening to **another** song, or still **STROKING** your cat, getting steadily **more** and **more STRESSED**, but avoiding doing the one thing that will take your stress away – **STARTING YOUR HOMEWORK**.

This is called **'PROCRASTINATION'** and everyone does it. **But why?** Again, it's all down to **chemicals** in the brain.

Why the wait?

You know you will feel **BETTER** as soon as your homework is done, so why don't you do it straight away? The answer to this lies in a part of your brain called the **'LIMBIC SYSTEM'**.

The decision to do your homework is made by your **prefrontal cortex**, the part of your brain that **PLANS** things like **WHEN** you get your homework done.

The **LIMBIC SYSTEM** is the part of your brain that will **REWARD** you with that **GOOD FEELING** when you get your homework **done**.

The problem with **PROCRASTINATION** is that when you listen to your favourite song or do whatever it is that is **stopping** you doing what you need to get done, your **limbic system** gives you a **BOOST** of **DOPAMINE** anyway. Dopamine feels good. It helps to relieve that feeling of **BUILDING TENSION** about your

homework, so you listen to another song, which gets you another dose of dopamine, **and so the cycle continues**.

And the problem with the **prefrontal cortex** is that it can't make us do what it wants. **We can just ignore it**. Your prefrontal cortex knows better, it wants to do **BETTER**, but the rest of your brain wants to do what feels good right now and so you **stay where you are**. This is called **'short-term mood repair'** and it is a cycle that is **HARD TO BREAK**.

Can you override it? You can! THANK GOODNESS. If people couldn't override it, we would all be sitting watching **CAT VIDEOS** on our tablets while the world **CRUMBLED** around us. In fact, that's **not true** because nobody would ever have **BOTHERED** to invent the **tablet** or **YouTube** or even have **domesticated cats** and taught them to walk across a **PIANO**.

Instead we would still be sitting doing whatever it was **PREHISTORIC MAN** did to **stop** him from going out hunting or starting that pesky cave painting he'd been meaning to get around to.

So, what you need instead is... **TIME TRAVEL!**

Wait! **Is that even possible?** Surely not? Also, if you can't get off the sofa and start your homework, it's a bit of a STRETCH to rustle up a **TIME MACHINE**.

Don't panic. You don't need an actual time machine. Psychologists call the technique time travel, probably to make it sound more **EXCITING**, but it's just your **IMAGINATION** that travels in time. Psychologists advise people who are struggling to get going on a **DIFFICULT TASK** to imagine how **GREAT** they will feel when they have finished it. Completing a task not only gives you a **bigger** dose of **FEEL-GOOD BRAIN CHEMICALS** than watching the next episode of your favourite show, it also gets rid of all the **ANXIETY** you had about not wanting to start it.

Do you know what also works? Being **SHOUTED** at by your parents. Eventually they get so **LOUD** that you can't hear the music anyway.

Still, for **HOMEWORK** today you just have to read something and reading is pretty **MIRACULOUS** itself.

Hit the books!

So, how does it even work? This thing you're doing right now – **reading?**

How are those words on a page able to give you **INSTRUCTIONS**? Or these words? How are you able to decode the **BLACK MARKS** typed into a computer, months, or even years ago and **UNDERSTAND** what they mean?

One of the most **INCREDIBLE** things about reading is that it's like **telepathy** and time travel all at once. I am able to think **something** and **write it down** and there you are, **months** or even **years** later able to decode the shapes I wrote down and

know **EXACTLY** what it was I was **THINKING** in my brain.

Read all about it!

As you **read** these words, you can feel your eyes moving across the page, probably from **LEFT TO RIGHT**, (unless you're reading this book in Arabic or Hebrew, in which case you're reading right to left. Best to check: are you reading this book in Arabic or Hebrew? Because you've been reading it backwards otherwise). As you read, your eyes jerk backwards and forwards, SUBCONSCIOUSLY checking if they have missed any **SUBTLE SHAPES**.

CORNEA

The light from the page shines into your eyes through your **cornea** (the clear sticky-outy bumps on the front of your eyeballs) into the pupil, where it is focused by the **LENS** onto the back wall of the eye, or **RETINA**. The retina is covered with LIGHT-SENSITIVE nerve cells called **'rods** and **cones'**. There are lots of them – each eye has approximately **120 million rods and 7 million cones**.

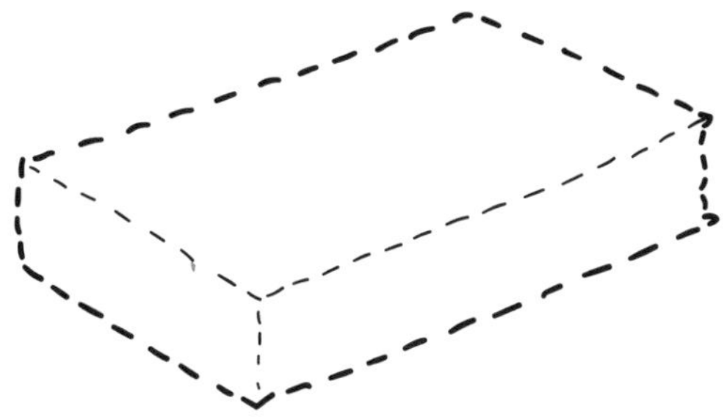

Rods and cones are very **SPECIAL** types of nerve cell that are able to convert light into **electrical** nerve signals.

Rods are sensitive to **black** and white and are also **important** in seeing the **SHAPE** or **OUTLINE** of an object, such as a **BOOK** or a **LETTER** in a word.

Cones are SENSITIVE to the colour of light. Three colours in fact. There are three different types of cone, one each for red light, blue light and green light, and together they allow us to see all the colours of the **RAINBOW** and lots of subtle shades in between.

The nerve signals from the rods and cones pass along the optic nerve to the brain where we interpret the **PICTURE**. The brain is constantly interpreting these signals and **TIDYING THEM UP** to make a sensible picture.

For a start, the image arrives **UPSIDE DOWN** because of the way the lens in our eye throws the LIGHT onto the **retina**.

This is the picture of the world we can really see. Just look at yourself in the back of a spoon. That's how your eye sees the world all the time apart from the bulge in the middle that makes your nose look huge.

So, **maybe**, just **maybe**, the world is actually **upside down** and we've been wrong all this time?

Well, **no**, of course, as we're constantly told by all our other **SENSES**. We don't need to have our eyes open to see tell which way is up. Just lift your arm and see where **GRAVITY** pulls it.

So, the brain, thankfully, steps in and **FLIPS** the picture round, so that up is **UP** and down is **DOWN**, and we know how to LOWER a **CUP OF WATER** onto a table.

We've even tried **TESTING** this by wearing special glasses that turn the picture upside down **BEFORE** it reaches your eyes. Then your eye flips it over as normal, sends the information to the brain and the brain **AUTOMATICALLY** reverses it again. **And now the world looks upside down. HA!** Take that brain! We **FOOLED** you! Except... after about ten days of seeing an upside-down world, but (the important bit) all the other senses telling you it's the right way up, your brain just **STOPS** reversing the picture. And you're back to seeing the world **CORRECTLY** again. Even when you stop the experiment, take off the glasses and **confuse** the brain again, it only takes **a day** for it to start reversing the image as normal. The brain is quite smart.

So, how does reading work, then?

Scientists studying how we read have found out that our brains actually recognize the words on the page as pictures. When the signals from your eyes reach your brain, they are processed by a part of your brain called the **'VISUAL WORD FORM AREA'**, which is just behind your left ear. When you are a **baby**, this part of your brain helps you to **RECOGNIZE** shapes and **DISTINGUISH** one face from another. As you learn to read, this area becomes responsible for recognizing the shapes of words and **CONNECTING** them to their meaning.

Want to see how good the brain is at using this shape recognition? **Try reading this**:

The fnuny tihng aoubt raednig is taht you can sitll udnrestnad wrdos eevn wehn tehy are all mddueled up.

The words in that sentence were **MUDDLED**, but at same time it wasn't **too hard** to read, because the first and last letter of the words were the **same**, only the middle got jumbled up, so your brain could skip over them, **DISTINGUISHING** their **basic shapes** without really noticing anything off.

Similarly, we can read the **same words** in different **FONTS**, and **DIFFERENT** handwriting, **EXCEPT** when the handwriting is **really**, **really BAD**.

We're basically saying the the brain is very clever. It's so clever it can skip over extra words it knows aren't important, without getting confused – like it did **JUST ONE SENTENCE AGO**. Did you spot the mistake?

Can you hear me?

Scientists have also **DISCOVERED** that reading transforms all writing into **AUDIO BOOKS** without you even having to open your mouth.

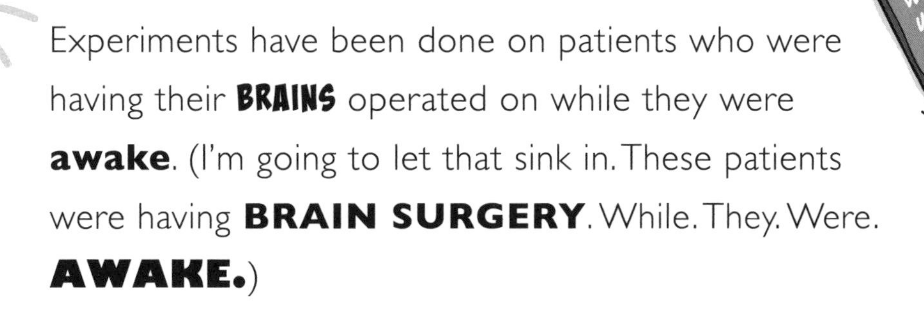

Experiments have been done on patients who were having their **BRAINS** operated on while they were **awake**. (I'm going to let that sink in. These patients were having **BRAIN SURGERY**. While. They. Were. **AWAKE.**)

Brain surgeons, otherwise known as '**neurosurgeons**', perform some surgeries on patients' brains while they are awake, so they can **monitor** how their patients are responding. They ask the patient **questions** and make them perform **MENTAL TASKS** (and even play musical instruments!) while they are **OPERATING** to make sure they don't cause any damage to parts of the brain that controls things such as speech or movement.

These **EXPERIMENTS** discovered that when they were asked to read some things, the patients' brains were **ACTIVE** in the **same area** whether they read words **out loud** or silently. This part, towards the front of the brain, known as **'Broca's area'**, is associated with speech. Broca's area responds to the words as if it was actually producing the **SOUNDS** of the words inside the reader's brain.

So now I know you can hear me... do you want to play some games?

I think you've earned it after all that **HOMEWORK**,

and if anyone asks, tell them we're still doing BRAIN SCIENCE.

PEW, PEW, PEW!

I love video games.

You do all sorts of things in a video game, without leaving the **comfort of your own home**. You can **INVADE NEW WORLDS**, *DRIVE FAST CARS* or even play in the **WORLD CUP FINAL**. Of course, you're doing none of these things **really**; and yet the **EXPERIENCE** is possibly **AS EXCITING** and **THRILLING** as the real thing, although we might have to wait until you're a little **OLDER** and start driving race cars, winning World Cups and invading new worlds in real life, then

you can tell us.

Video games are an INCREDIBLE mix of smart technology and **CLEVER BRAIN SCIENCE** combining to make a totally **FAKE** experience as REAL as possible. Video game machines are now so powerful that the brain of the computer, the CPU (central processing unit), can do up to **200,000 million** calculations per SECOND, a lot of it spent drawing the INCREDIBLE artificial worlds you see in every direction, while you spin around wondering where to go next to **SHOOT AT ALIENS**.

Even the controllers use some pretty **nifty software**. You might have a controller that can tell when you're *TILTING* it, so that you can DRIVE round corners smoothly. To do that it uses a device called an **ACCELEROMETER**, a big word for a **TINY**, tiny machine that measures **SUDDEN** changes in direction.

In some ways, it's not that different to

how our senses tell us which way up we are. We have tubes in our ears called the **'SEMI-CIRCULAR CANALS'**, because, *ahem*, they are semi-circular tubes filled with **LIQUID**.

There are three of them, because we live in a **3D world**, where we can move **up** and **down**, **left** and **right**, **forward** and **back**, in any combination, of course. Therefore, there's a **TUBE** that tells us we're **moving up** and **down**, a **TUBE** that tells us if we're **going left** or **right** and well, I think you're getting the idea here...

Similarly, the **ACCELEROMETER** in your controller can tell when you've *TILTED* or **twisted** your head, and what **direction** you've gone in. That way you can use the controller to **steer a car**, for example.

The even more **EXCITING** bit is when we put **ACCELEROMETERS** in **VIRTUAL**

REALITY (VR) HEADSETS. In a VR headset, there is a screen for **each eye** and the picture changes according to how you move your head. You **tilt up** and the computer makes the picture tilt up at the **same speed**, and so on. However, now both your **EARS** and the **ACCELEROMETERS** are tracking the same movement! And that can cause some **huge problems...**

If the accelerometers **aren't** doing their job QUICKLY and **ACCURATELY** enough, the **computer-generated** picture your eyes see will be **DIFFERENT** from what your ears have told your brain to expect. And that confusion between what you **see** and what you **feel...** well, that has the unfortunate result of causing **DIZZINESS** and **SUDDEN VOMITING**. Which will be bad for

your **HIGH SCORE**, and your sofa. How FAST do the screens have to be to keep up with your EARS? Well, if the picture is **slower** by even **5 to 10 thousandths of a second**, you may start getting that QUEASY feeling. This is faster than you can even see it happening, but it's enough to trigger a **YUCKY RESPONSE**.

APPARENTLY, this is particularly bad for children **aged two to 12**, which is bad news for **you**, but it improves a lot after that.

But while the tech is cool, what is this doing to your brain?

You've probably heard grown-ups saying that playing video games all day is **not very good for you**; it will **NUMB** your brain and **RUIN** your eyesight.

Some of the **FEARS** about gaming have been found to be **EXAGGERATED**.

For example, is too much staring at screens really bad for your eyesight? **Neuroscientists** have looked into this and found that the **OPPOSITE** is true. By testing groups of people – some who played **NO** video games **versus** gamers who played up to **15 hours a week** – they found that the gamers' eyesight was **CONSIDERABLY BETTER** than those who did no gaming at all. Probably from all the searching the horizon for **ENEMIES**.

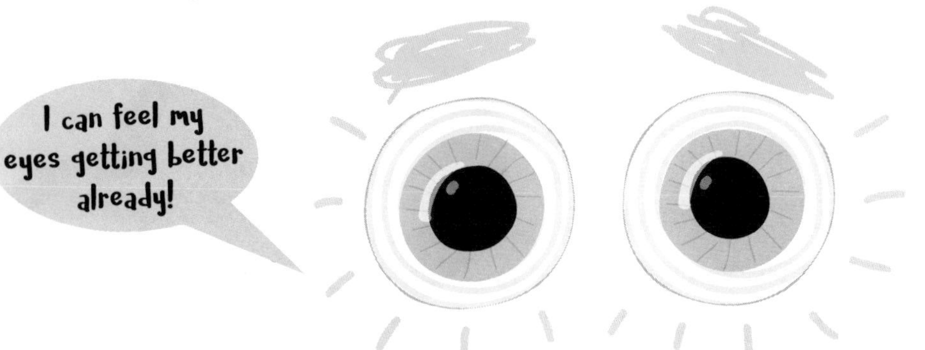

Or does playing video games give you a short attention span?

Nope. Again, they measured this in a lab (scientists have specific tests for measuring attention) and they found gamers who played **ACTION GAMES** actually did **BETTER** than those who played no games at all. They even scanned the **BRAINS** of gamers and discovered the parts of the brain that are involved with **ATTENTION** are all more active in the brains of gamers than non-gamers.

Gaming can be **ADDICTIVE** though, due to those same reward centres in your brain also linked with **procrastination**. You play the game; your brain releases **REWARD CHEMICALS**, so you keep playing. Game designers are aware of this and put **BRAIN-CHEMICAL-STIMULATING** features in their games to keep you playing.

Have you ever noticed how video games offer lots of regular, **COLOURFUL REWARDS?** Gold coins, level-ups, new equipment **'unlocked'**, lots of ding-**ding-**

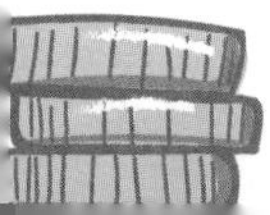
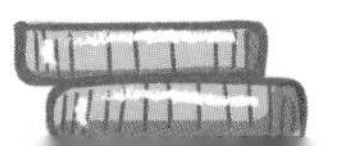
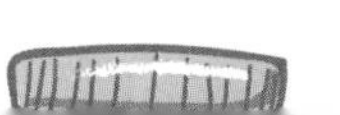
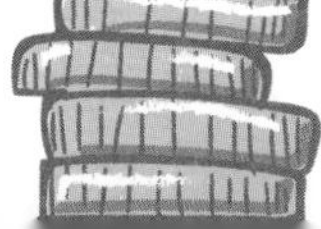
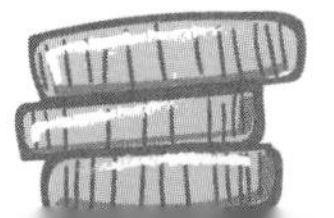

ding noises. It's all part of the process of teasing **DOPAMINE** into your brain to keep you constantly rewarded. It feels **GOOD** to play games because they are built to make you feel good.

That's why you'd **LIKE** to play video games **ALL DAY**, and you can now point to the benefits to your **EYE SIGHT** and **ATTENTION**, but **should** you play video games all day? **Well, NO,** of course you shouldn't. For a start, it can leave you with loads of those **FIGHT-OR-FLIGHT CHEMICALS** fizzing round your system with nowhere to go, which isn't great for your **HEALTH**, or your **MOOD**.

Also, playing video games all day isn't good for you, in the same way as doing **ANYTHING** all day isn't good for you. There's just a bit too much **SITTING AROUND**.

At some point, it's time to **get up** and **out**

and **RUN AROUND** (or swim, or dance, or play wheelchair basketball or whatever). And, yet again, your brain will **THANK YOU** for it...

Get out!

If **SPORTS video games** are your thing, what's the difference between playing a **NAIL-BITING WORLD CUP FINAL** on your **console** and **heading outside** with your mates for a good kickabout? After all, both get your **HEART RACING**...

This is true. The **EXCITEMENT** you feel when you are playing a video game is **real**: your body releases hormones and **NEUROTRANSMITTERS**, **REWARDING** you for

good play and raising your pulse so you can perform at your **BEST**. But it's not the same as the **HEART POUNDING** you feel when you have been running around outside for 20 minutes.

EXERCISE helps you to **build muscle** and **IMPROVE STAMINA**, so it works your heart muscle, which has to beat faster to pump the **blood** that supplies all

the other **hard-working** muscles with everything they need to keep running: things such as **sugar** and **OXYGEN**.

Your heart does this because it can tell it is under **STRESS**. The great thing about exercise over other forms of **EXCITEMENT-INDUCING** activities, such as gaming though, is that your brain releases other chemicals to

counteract this stress. Your body NEEDS the stress chemicals to do what it needs to do to perform well on the pitch – to *RUN FASTER*, **jump higher.** But unlike being chased by a sabre-toothed tiger, **THIS IS FUN!**

Your body knows that this is **good** for it and so to reward you for your **HARD WORK**, it releases reward chemicals, such as a protein called **brain-derived neurotrophic factor**, or **BDNF**, which is more fun than reading the name. This **CLEVER** protein helps **PROTECT** the brain from **STRESS** and repairs memory neurons that get a bit frazzled in all the **EXCITEMENT**. It is thought that **BDNF** is the reason you often feel so **relaxed** after a good workout. Your body has experienced stress, but it has **REPAIRED** itself.

Bliss bound

You may also have heard of another **REWARD NEUROTRANSMITTER** associated with exercise called **'ENDORPHINS'**. Super-fit people like to talk about something called an **'ENDORPHIN RUSH'**, which is the **HAPPY SENSATION** they get when they exercise really hard.

Basically, your body is designed to **EXERCISE**. It needs to move to stay **HEALTHY**, so it rewards you for your hard work on the pitch with a dose of **ENDORPHINS** that **REDUCE PAIN** (and sometimes exercising really hard can hurt) and make you feel **BLISSFULLY HAPPY**. Who doesn't like to feel happy?

That's not all. Studies have shown that physical exercise can make you **FITTER**, better able to fight disease, improve your confidence and help your **MOOD**. And fear not, if you think you'll miss all those **'fight or flight'** chemicals you got while playing video games, just release a **SABRE-TOOTHED TIGER** into the garden at the same time.

Exciting enough for you?

Let's Get
Out of Here!

This **ordinary** day we're living today is just a bit too **'ordinary'** though, isn't it?

I mean, we could choose any day of the year, so why not just click our fingers and choose something a little more... **EXTRAORDINARY**. Maybe today didn't start with a trip on the bus to school. Maybe today started... on an **AEROPLANE**.

You're off on your holidays!

Ready for take-off?

As you're sitting in your **comfy** aeroplane seat, wondering which **MOVIE** to watch, **KICKING** the seat in front of you (please don't really do that!), seeing if all your **STUFF** will fit into the elasticated pocket, and deciding if you'll have the **CHICKEN** or the **FISH**, it might be nice just to take a moment and reflect on what a proper **MIRACLE** planes are.

Take a look around. **Look at all the passengers!** If you are on a **jumbo jet**, you might be sitting alongside over **400 PEOPLE**, all of you sitting in a metal box travelling at nearly **575 MILES** (930 km) per hour **35,000 FEET** (10,000 km) above the ground. It might be more than **400 TONS** of weight, which is as **heavy** as, **oooohhh**, let me work it out... **LOADS OF ELEPHANTS**. And yet, unlike loads of elephants, **IT CAN FLY**.

This could work!

We have lift-off!

So, what makes it fly? Well, not the engines. Although they are pretty **USEFUL**. But if you strapped a jet engine to a bicycle it wouldn't fly. It would just go forward **really, really fast**.

The basic principle of the jet engine is the **SAME** as the engine in a car. Remember all that **EXPLODING PLANKTON** that drove us to school earlier? The jet engine also combines **fuel** with **air** and **IGNITES** it to release ENERGY to move the aeroplane forward. It just does this on a **massive** scale.

A **FAN** at the front pulls **COOL AIR** inside the engine.

A **SECOND FAN** squashes or compresses this air around **eight times** smaller, which makes the air really **HOT**. If you squash a gas, you basically pack its **molecules** closer together and that means the molecules **CRASH** into each other more often. These collisions produce **HEAT**.

Meanwhile a fuel called **'kerosene'** is injected into the **COMBUSTION CHAMBER** where it mixes with the hot compressed air and then **BOOM!** It **BURNS FEROCIOUSLY**.

When the kerosene **BURNS**, it produces a mixture of **HOT** exhaust gases, such as **carbon dioxide** and **water vapour**.

These hot exhaust gases **PUSH** their way out of the combustion chamber by **SPINNING** through a turbine while **COOLING** down and then out of the jet engine through a much **smaller** opening at the back of the engine. That jet of air is what **DRIVES** the engine, and the plane, *FORWARD*.

Feel the force!

You know when you're in the garden and your dad is using the **HOSEPIPE** and he has to tie something up, so you're given the hosepipe to **hold**, and your dad specifically says, **'Do not spray your brother!'**, **BUT** your brother is totally not expecting it so it's the **PERFECT TIME** to spray him, but he's also a little too far away to get easily, so you put your **thumb** over the end of the hose, which makes the hole smaller, forcing the water out with greater pressure, and this is the most important bit, he gets soaked? **Well, that's what a jet engine does.**

The gases **EXITING** the jet engine are moving TWICE as fast as the gases that entered the engine. It's this increase in speed that pushes the aircraft forward.

Okay, brilliant! We are hurtling down the runway at a ridiculous speed. How do we get **off the ground**, preferably **BEFORE** we run out of runway?

How wings work: a quiz for parents and teachers

The **engine** makes the plane go *FORWARD*, but it's the **WINGS** that make it **TAKE OFF**. In fact, once you hit a certain speed driving forward down that runway, those wings are going to start lifting the plane. Wings just gotta fly. **It's what they were built to do**.

Before we explain how, let's remind ourselves of what they are flying **through**. We often forget that we are walking around at the bottom of an ocean of gases, called our **ATMOSPHERE**. The air sits on top of you, going up as far as 120 km (74.5 miles). (The height at which a space-craft returning to Earth might begin to feel the effects of passing through the atmosphere, or 'burning up' as it's called. At any time, there might be a

ton of air sitting above your head, although you don't feel a **ton weight** on you since all that air **isn't** pushing downwards at the same time; it's a GAS, so it is *PUSHING* in all directions all the time.

There is some **downward** pressure, but we're so used to it we don't even notice. In fact, if you could dive down to a depth of **10 METRES** (32 feet) in the sea, the pressure would double. That is to say, 10 metres of water above you has as much pressure as the entire atmosphere.

Nonetheless, we swim in a sea of air, and planes use that air to *PUSH* themselves off the ground.

A lot of people have been told the **wrong** reason for how planes do this though, so this is good opportunity to QUIZ THEM. Find the SMARTEST adult you know and say, **"How do plane wings work?"**

They will probably have been told this: when the wing moves through the air, it splits it into two parts – the air above the wing and the air below the wing, like so:

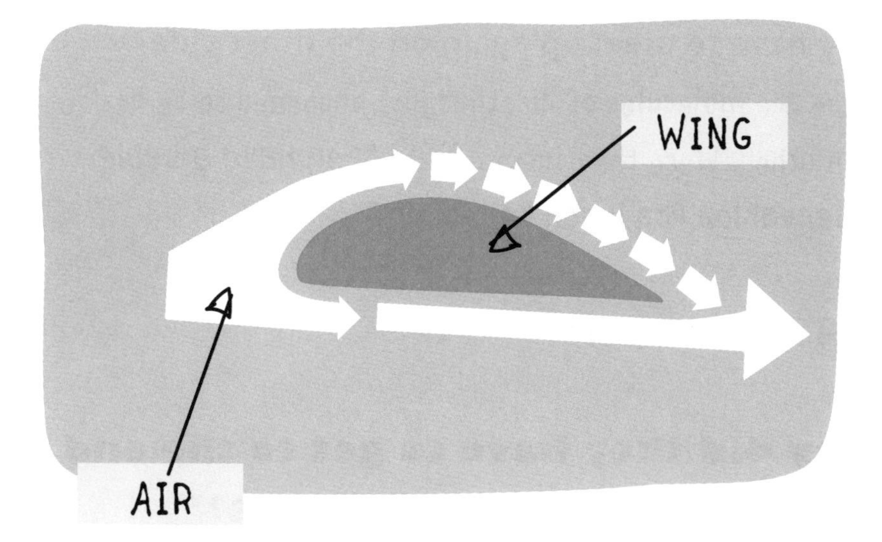

The **SHAPE** of the wing means that the air **above** the wing has to travel FURTHER than the air **below** the wing in order to meet up again at the end of the wing, and so it has to *SPEED UP*. So, you have **FASTER** air above the wing than below. That means the air pressure is **bigger** below the wing and so the wing 'LIFTS' towards the lower pressure.

Then your **mum** or **dad** will rub their hands, as if to say, "**JOB DONE!**" And you will say, "**Why does it matter that the journey is longer above the wing?** Why do they have to meet up again on the other side? These are molecules of air, that just happened to be beside each other. Were they friends? *Did they have a table reservation for lunch together?*

WHY, PARENT?

Why did they have to get to the end of the wing at the same time?"

And the grown-up will **emm** and **ahh** and then send you to **BED** or **out of the room**.

This idea that the **AIR MOLECULES** were in a mad rush to meet up again with their **MATES** has become one of those **STRANGE** things that's been taught **over** and **over** again. It's obvious when you think about it, but the air on the top of the wing has **NO IDEA** what's happening to the air beneath it, and two **DIFFERENT** things are happening.

Below the wing, air is being **pushed** down by the angle of the wing, particularly by the bit at the end. The air above the wing **rises** above the bump and then *RUSHES* down the slope **faster** and **FASTER** to fill the space.

The result is that both the air **above** and **below** is sent *SPEEDING* downwards, creating a huge 'DOWNWASH' of air and when something is pushed down, something else must be pushed UP. The thing pushed up is the WING, so it RISES, carrying the PLANE with it.

Those wings just gotta fly.

As the aircraft CLIMBS to its **CRUISING ALTITUDE**, it moves into THINNER AIR and less air around the plane means LESS AIR PRESSURE, which affects your journey in a number of ways, some of them quite **PAINFUL.**

As I said earlier, when you're **WALKING** around on the ground you're probably **not aware** of the **PRESSURE** of the air around you at all. Why would you be? It **seems** to be just the right pressure to **BREATHE** even though you actually have an entire **ATMOSPHERE** of gases sitting on top of you at all times. **That's quite a lot of gases.**

As you rise above sea level, the air becomes **LESS DENSE** and there is **LESS PRESSURE** because there is **LESS AIR** pressing down on it from above.

This causes **PROBLEMS** in any spaces that have trapped air inside them, such as your **EARS**. As the aircraft **climbs** into the sky you might feel a strange, perhaps painful, **SENSATION** in your ears. This is the air inside your ears pushing against your **EARDRUM**. The air inside your ears is at a higher pressure than the air outside because it is **STILL** at the pressure it was down at sea level. This higher-pressure air pushes your eardrum **OUTWARDS,** which is why it is **PAINFUL**.

Feel the squeeze!

To fix this, simply **pinch your nose**, **CLOSE YOUR MOUTH** and **try** to gently **BREATHE OUT**. This pushes air from your lungs into **tiny tubes**, known as **eustachian tubes**, at the back of your nose that connect to your inner ear and **EQUALIZES** the air pressure again.

As you land, it may happen **again**, but this time in the **OPPOSITE** direction. As the aircraft gets closer to sea level the air pressure INCREASES, pushing your eardrum inwards. **There's that pain again! Time to do the pinching thing.** You can also do **exaggerated swallowing**, or SUCKING, or anything that **MOVES** the air around. Airlines used to hand out **boiled sweets** to help this, which weren't a cure 100 per cent of the time, **BUT HEY!** At least you got a **SWEET**.

The **EFFECTS** you felt in your **EARS** were happening all around the plane too, of course. The **HIGHER** we go the THINNER the air is; if you were breathing the air outside when your plane was at **35,000 feet** (10,000 metres) **cruising altitude**, there just wouldn't be enough **OXYGEN** in each gulp to keep you alive. In about a minute, you'd be **UNCONSCIOUS**, and not long after, you'd be **DEAD**.

So, this is why we say planes are at **'CABIN PRESSURE'**. We keep the metal tube with all the people in it at an air pressure that is **HEALTHY** to breathe, but not the same as down on the ground, because that would put too much **STRAIN** on the **plane**. Basically we fly at **35,000 FEET** (10,000 metres) but the inside of cabin feels like you're at about **6,500 FEET** (2,000 metres).

If you don't **believe me**, next time you're on a plane, do this experiment. Take a plastic bottle of water with you, then when you're in the middle of the flight drink it all and close the bottle, and pop it in your bag. When you're back on the ground, and the air pressure is back to **normal**, take out the bottle and see how much it has **CRUMPLED INWARDS**. This is because the pressure inside the bottle is much **smaller** then outside, so the bottle gets SQUISHED.

So, if there is less outside than inside... where does the air come from?

Some people still think that when you get on a plane you just breathe the SAME AIR **round** and **round** until the plane lands. Actually, aeroplanes have **CLEANER** air than most offices, because they suck **FRESH** air in through the engines, but before it gets to the **EXPLODEY** bit they take some of it to circulate through the cabin. It's not as rich in **OXYGEN** as the air at ground level so it can feel a little **STALE**, but it's **CLEAN**, and contrary to popular myth they don't just circulate the other passengers' **SNEEZES** and **FARTS** for the entire trip.

And if you're wondering why we don't just fly **lower** and save ourselves all this **HASSLE**, planes used to, but as well as being more efficient for jet engines, this new height has the massive **ADVANTAGE** of being above the weather. **STORMS** and **choppy clouds** usually occur in the **DENSER** air below 9,000 metres (3,000 feet) **(called the troposphere)**. Planes used to have to travel through all that and so flying used to be a lot more... **up and down**, than it is these days. That's why you'll find a long paper bag in the seat pocket in front of you. It's a **'SICK'** bag; in case of a **BAD TUMMY EMERGENCY**, and they were a necessary supply on long flights when the passengers had to endure being thrown about by regular storms and **TURBULENCE**, and when the **smell** of the **FUEL** from the engine was in their noses the entire way.

Now, we **glide** serenely **ABOVE** all that but even though sick bags are rarely used today, they remain available as a reminder of a **ROUGHER ERA**, and also... **JUST IN CASE**.

Feel the heat!

Finally, you've arrived, and it's time to ENJOY the heat. But why can't it be **THIS WARM** at home?

WHERE ON EARTH?

The answer to this lies in where you **LIVE** on planet Earth and where you have gone on **HOLIDAY**.

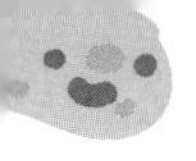

If you live in the **United Kingdom** or **Ireland** and you have gone on holiday somewhere warm, you have almost certainly flown **SOUTH**.

The United Kingdom and Ireland are in the **northern hemisphere**, or top half of the planet. As you move south, the weather gets **WARMER** the closer you get to the midpoint between the **northern** and **southern hemispheres**: **THE EQUATOR**. Light from the **SUN**, hits **THE EQUATOR** straight on because the **SUN** is directly above it. As you move north or south the curvature of the Earth means you begin to 'tilt' away from the **SUN'S** light and so receive less **energy** (heat) from it.

Feel the burn!

As we've mentioned before, almost all the energy we have on this planet has come to us from the **SUN**. Like all stars, the Sun is **HOT** because its **MASSIVE** size means all the **hydrogen atoms** at the centre are SQUEEZED together so hard by gravity that they turn into helium, which releases huge amounts of **ENERGY**, that radiates out from the Sun across space as **SUNLIGHT**.

That's the **HEAT** we feel on our faces when we're on **HOLIDAY** somewhere warm: the released energy from **hydrogen** being smashed together to make helium.

This **ENERGY** gets sent out as **ELECTROMAGNETIC WAVES**, which we spoke about earlier: **wobbles** in that electromagnetic field which **invisibly** surrounds us all the time.

The waves, which come in lots of **different SIZES**, are sent out in packets called **'PHOTONS'** or 'LIGHT PARTICLES', but in reality they are just **wobbles** in the electromagnetic field.

If this whole idea seems weird and a bit difficult, **DON'T BE DISCOURAGED!** Big grown-up scientists have struggled to get their heads around it for **hundreds of years**; and plenty of big grown-ups **still** don't get it.

There are different **WAVELENGTHS** of these little packets (short and punchy and filled with energy, or long and drawn-out lower energy) so the different wobbles behave differently, which means we can use them differently, too. Some of them can be used to **HEAT** your dinner in a **MICROWAVE**, others can play your favourite **music** on the **RADIO**.

Another amazing use of these waves: do you remember photosynthesis from earlier? Plants are able to use this **SUNLIGHT** to transform **carbon dioxide** and **water** into sugar, which is the first step in producing all the food on Earth. Which we can agree is both **BRILLIANT**, and **HELPFUL** at lunchtime.

Some **WAVES** activate the rods and cones in your **EYES**, as VISIBLE LIGHT. Others, called **infrared waves**, are just outside the range we can see and can carry **HEAT**.

It's infrared that makes you feel warm in the Sun. It isn't strong enough to **BURN** your skin, but it can cause you to **OVERHEAT** and **SWEAT**. Make sure to drink **LOTS** of **WATER** to stay hydrated.

It's not ALL good news

However, some of these light particles **CAN** burn you.

If you've ever forgotten to put on **SUNSCREEN**, you may have noticed your skin turn **RED** and become hot and **painful** to touch. This is caused by a particular type of radiation from the Sun called **ultraviolet**, or **UV radiation**.

Ultraviolet radiation is also just outside the range of light we can see, but on the more **ENERGETIC** end of the scale than infrared. It also makes the molecules in your skin cells **shake**. But ultraviolet radiation's **shorter WAVELENGTH** and higher frequency shakes the molecules in your skin so fast that it can cause them to kick away **electrons** and even break the bonds between the molecules.

In the heart of your **SKIN CELLS**, and all of the cells of the body, is your **DNA**, which is like the body's **INSTRUCTION MANUAL** that tells the cells how to **build themselves**.

These are the molecules that the **ultraviolet radiation** can damage.

When **UV** radiation **breaks down** the molecules in the skin's cell, the cells signal the body to allow more **BLOOD** to flow to the skin to help cool it down. This is what makes your skin **RED**.

Sometimes, though, the damage can be **SO SEVERE** that it can **KILL** the cell itself, which is what causes your skin to **BLISTER** and **PEEL**.

LUCKILY, our body has ways of **repairing** the **DNA**

DAMAGE, but if exposure to the Sun is **frequent**, it makes it more likely that the damage to DNA will result in **permanent changes** in the sequence of the DNA molecule, which is known as a **'MUTATION'**. So the instructions in the manual get mixed up, and they make the **wrong** sort of cell instead. That might potentially lead to a very **DANGEROUS** disease, called **CANCER**.

Your body has a way of trying to **PROTECT** itself from the Sun though. When your skin is exposed to the Sun, it produces a brown pigment called **'MELANIN'**, which is able to **ABSORB** some of the Sun's radiation. This pigment is what gives your skin its **COLOUR** and is why after you have spent a lot of time in Sun, your skin gets **DARKER**. Far from being a healthy holiday souvenir, a **TAN** is a sign that you have **DAMAGED** your skin. The tan is the body's **EMERGENCY** attempt to **PROTECT** itself.

People with **DARKER** skin have **more MELANIN** than people with LIGHTER skin, which does give more protection from some of the sun's rays, **BUT** however much melanin you have in your skin, you are still at RISK from **CANCER**, so everyone needs to wear **SUNSCREEN**.

But wait, what if you go in the **WATER? That cools you down!** Surely it'll stop the Sun **BURNING** you?

Hmmmm.

Time for a dip

No, even though the **POOL**, **OCEAN** or **POND** feels pretty **COOL** on your skin, all it is doing is **lowering the temperature**. It isn't doing anything to help your cells from the bombardment of **KILLER RAYS FROM SPACE**. In fact, if you are in the water you can even get damage from the UV waves reflecting up off the surface, increasing the risk of burning.

So, are you safe **UNDERWATER**? Well, you can obviously see that **normal** VISIBLE LIGHT reaches the **BOTTOM** of the swimming pool. **UV** rays aren't as good as visible light at getting to the depths, particularly in the **DIRTIER** water of the oceans, so you're pretty safe at about **10 metres** (32 feet) **down**. **How long can you hold your breath? Otherwise, yep, pop on that suncream.**

Do you remember that we mentioned **10 metres** (32 feet) of **WATER** before? Back when we spoke about **AIR PRESSURE** in planes, we said that all the air sitting on your head was putting **PRESSURE** on it. If you want to **double** the pressure on your head, just **SWIM** down 10 metres. **120 km** (74.5 miles) **of atmosphere** has the **SAME** pressure as **10 metres of water!**

Long before you get to **10 metres** though, you'll have had to **POP** your **EARS** just like you did on the plane, for the **exact same reason** you popped them while the plane was landing. As the pressure increases outside, the air pressure in your **INNER EAR** isn't enough to stop the eardrum being pushed in, and this causes **PAIN**. Scuba divers have **TANKS** and **WETSUITS** and **weight belts** and **fancy expensive watches** that work down to **200 metres** (656 feet) – but they won't get anywhere unless they can **HOLD** their nose and clear their ears instead. And there is definitely **NO** boiled sweet for this trip.

One of the most fun parts of **swimming** in the sea is **bobbing** up and down in the waves as they come **CRASHING** in to shore. Strangely, though, even though the waves are clearly travelling forward towards the beach, it's difficult to get pulled along by them. More often they just **LIFT YOU** and **drop you**, which is fun, but something definitely seems to have passed by while you were moving. **WHAT WAS THAT?**

Waves are caused by wind, when the molecules of **air** drag along the molecules of **WATER** as they WHIZZ past. That transfers energy to the water, which becomes a **WAVE**. When waves move across the ocean towards the shore, it can appear that it is **WATER** moving across the ocean – **but it isn't at all**. A wave doesn't **SWIM** through the water like a shark's fin driving forward. The wave is just the **energy** passing forward, and the water just moves **UP** and **down** to help it along.

Yeah, this is another one of those concepts **LOADS** of grown-ups don't get. But you'll get it because you can stand in the sea as a **WAVE** approaches, suddenly get **LIFTED** and **dropped**, and turn around to watch the wave carrying on **WITHOUT YOU** or the water around you.

It doesn't go on forever though...

When waves meet the shore, something very **INTERESTING** happens.

When the water is **shallower** than half the distance between two waves **(the wavelength)**, friction

between the water molecules at the bottom of wave and the ocean floor **slow** the bottom of the wave down. This means that the top of the wave is moving *FASTER* than the bottom of the **WAVE** and so the wave starts to **TOPPLE** over, in the same way as you can **TRIP** while running. Your feet come to a **(SUDDEN)** stop, whereas your body is still **moving** at the speed you were running, which causes you to **STUMBLE**.

As the water becomes even **shallower**, the wave reaches **BREAKING POINT**. The top of the wave is moving so much faster than the bottom that it begins to **BEND** and **SPILL** over the top. This is called **BREAKING**. Again, this is like **TRIPPING**, but when you land flat on your face.

Urgh, I'm so clumsy

Floating around

So, **SUNCREAM** on, **get in** and say hello to the **WONDERFUL REFRESHING WATER.** That's better. Lie back and relax. Let the ocean take the **weight** of your feet as you **float** and **drift** along the shore. Not a care in the world. Time to relax and think of the **big questions**. Like, it's **obvious** how your breakfast cereal floats, or how a football floats, because those things are LIGHT and clearly LESS DENSE than water, so they float, **but...** How is it then, when your body feels pretty solid, and is made up of around **60 PER CENT WATER** and lots of other stuff, some of which is denser than water, that you float on the ocean so **EASILY?**

The answer is in the **WATER** – specifically the answer is the **SALT**, which is in the seawater. When salt dissolves in water it increases its **density**, and this means your body, and other things, float more easily in **SALTWATER** than they do in **FRESH WATER**, such as in a lake or pool. Try it the next time you are at a destination with the sea and a pool. **Where do you find it easiest to float?**

One place you can experience this better than anywhere else is in the **Dead Sea**, which isn't actually a sea at all, but a **SALTWATER LAKE** in the Middle East.

In most oceans the salt is about **3.5 per cent** of saltwater, which means that a litre of seawater will contain 3.5 grams of salt. The Dead Sea is much, much **SALTIER**. The water in the Dead Sea can reach concentrations of around **34 per cent salt** (which is very, very salty indeed). This makes the water so dense that it is really easy to **float** in. So easy that you can lie in it reading a newspaper. In fact, it can be hard to stand up in the water, as no matter how hard you try, you can't get your feet to sink to the bottom. Similarly, it's nearly **IMPOSSIBLE** to dive under the surface of the Dead Sea, which is probably a **GOOD THING**, since the water is so **SALTY** that it can cause **CHEMICAL BURNS** and **POISONING** if you accidentally swallow any of it. There are no fish in the Dead Sea. **It's not called the Dead Sea for nothing...**

Buckets and spades, please!

What else is fun to do at the beach? Building a **SANDCASTLE**, of course. But not just any castle – the **biggest** and **BEST** castle this beach has ever seen!

Grab your bucket, fill it with sand, tip it over and get going!

Wait, what happened? That doesn't look much like the start of a castle, more a **SMALL HILL**.

Try it again, but this time go CLOSER to the **OCEAN** where the sand is **WETTER**. **Fill your bucket, pat down the sand and tip it over.**

THERE YOU GO! Now that's a **GREAT** start to the castle.

So, what's the **DIFFERENCE?** Why did the **WET** sand make a better castle than the **DRY** sand?

The **ANSWER** lies in **WATER MOLECULES**.

Sand needs just the right amount of **WATER** to be able to form into the **PERFECT SANDCASTLE**. **Sandcastle scientists** had long believed that the ideal ratio was one bucket of water to eight buckets of dry sand. However, recent research from the Laboratory of Physical Statistics in Paris has shockingly announced that the perfect figure might be closer to 1 per cent water and 99 per cent sand.

And yes, I said sandcastle scientists. Why not?

WATER MOLECULES sit between the grains of sand, clinging to them while forming little **BRIDGES** between the different **grains** with their strong

PLUS-MINUS BONDS. Remember them? Water is **POLAR**, so it likes to **JOIN UP** with other water molecules so that **pluses** get to meet **minuses** and **gently** hold on to them. Hence **SOAP** working, and **SURFACE TENSION**, and things getting **'WET'** and all the other **AMAZING** things water does. And now, the final triumph for water: **making better sandcastles**.

But **surely**, we should now add even more water because more water means more **plus–minus** bonds and that would mean a **STRONGER** castle. **Right?**

WRONG! The **SECRET** to a good castle is having **damp** rather than **SOPPING WET** sand. The thin layer of water between each grain of sand is what gives the castle its **STRENGTH**. When more water is added to the castle the water molecules between the grains of sand begin to **lose** their **stretchy-bridge** type structure and **CLING** to each other instead, forming **DROPLETS**. These droplets run through the grains of sand leaving a **SLOPPY MESS**.

Now you know the **PERFECT FORMULA**. You're going to build the **PERFECT CASTLE!** Oh wait, that took too long and the tide came in and **WASHED IT ALL AWAY**.

See? You **CAN** have **TOO MUCH WATER**.

I scream, you scream

You definitely deserve an **ICE CREAM** after all that **HARD WORK**.

A **TRIPLE SCOOP** of ice-cold ice cream. What could be better? Go on! Take a big bite! **YUM!**

WAIT! What's that feeling of **INTENSE** but **weird PAIN** building in your head?

Perhaps take **another bite** to take your mind off it. It really is the most **delicious** ice cream, isn't it? **AARGH! There it is again! What is it?** It's like it. **Wants. You. To. Stop. Eating. The. Ice. Cream.**

You have **BRAIN FREEZE.**

Actually, among **SCIENCE-Y** folks, brain freeze is officially called **'sphenopalatine ganglioneuralgia'**. Which is why everyone just calls it brain freeze instead.

There are lots of **BLOOD VESSELS** in your mouth and throat, including ones that lead up to your **BRAIN**. When you eat or drink something that is VERY COLD, like a **delicious ice cream**, you cause the temperature in the roof of your mouth to **drop** very quickly. Your brain finds this rapid change in temperature in the mouth **DISTRESSING**. Brain freeze is your body's way of telling you to **slow down** and give the blood vessels in your mouth time to **ADJUST** to the new **FROSTILY delicious** conditions.

Basically, the many **PAIN-RECEIVING** nerve cells interpret such a big change as pain and send **messages** to your brain that something **VERY WRONG** is happening in your mouth and must be **STOPPED**.

These **messages** are brought by the same nerves that inform the brain of **PAIN** in the **FACE**, so the brain interprets it as a pain in the **forehead**. Which is unfair since there is nothing wrong with your forehead **at all** and nothing you do to your forehead, like **rubbing it** or **WARMING IT** or **FROWNING VIOLENTLY**, will have any benefit at all.

INTERESTINGLY, did you know that unlike other parts of the body, the brain itself **cannot** feel pain? It has no pain receptors, so no headaches actually happen **IN** the brain. But that's not helping you very much here, sorry.

Best take a break. Try pressing your tongue to the roof of your mouth. Your tongue is filled with **blood vessels** too, carrying lots of **lovely warm blood**. This will help warm up the roof of your mouth. Sipping a **WARM DRINK** will help too, and then perhaps, maybe, eat your ice cream a bit more **slowly?**

A firework farewell

How best to round off this **MAGICAL DAY**? We've been going on and on about the **AMAZING** INVISIBLE things around you, but, for a treat, why not make something **REALLY VISIBLE** happen? Let's light up the sky with **sizzling** **REDS**,

YELLOWS, GREENS, **ORANGES** and **BLUES!** What better way to round off the perfect holiday than with an AMAZING

FIREWORK DISPLAY.

Fireworks are believed to have been invented in ancient China by a **CHINESE MONK** named **Li Tian**, to fend off **EVIL SPIRITS**. And, at their most basic, a firework is still just a mix of **chemicals** that **EXPLODE** when lit, and a fuse to delay that moment, until you've **RUN AWAY** a safe distance.

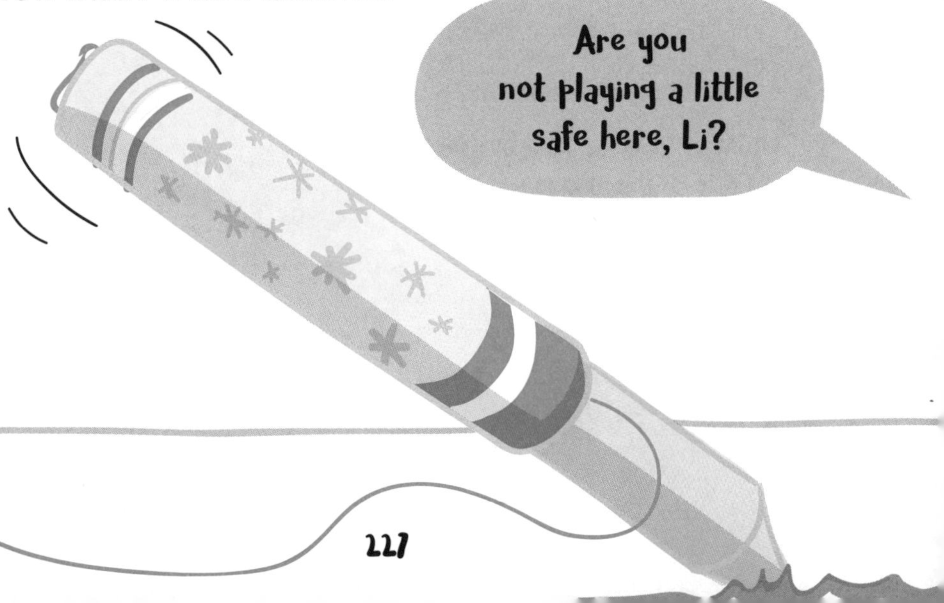

Are you not playing a little safe here, Li?

The chemical mix is called **'GUNPOWDER'**, which is just a mix of **sulphur**, **charcoal** and **POTASSIUM NITRATE**. This is the bit that acts really quickly.

The fuse of a firework is the **time delay**. Fuses are made of **FABRIC** string wrapped around a core of gunpowder that burns very **EASILY**. We light one end of the fuse and the **FLAME** travels along the length as the fabric **BURNS**. Then it meets the part of the firework called **the 'charge'**.

Why is it called 'the charge'?

Because when you light it, it all goes CHAAAAARRRRGGGE!

When the fuse **IGNITES** the charge, things start to happen **really**, **really** QUICKLY. The gunpowder in the charge ignites to produce gases and **HEAT**. The heat causes the gases to **expand** very quickly.

When gunpowder is ignited, the charcoal, potassium nitrate and sulphur **react** together to make new chemicals. What makes this so **SPECIAL** is that it is what we call an **'exothermic reaction'**. Exothermic reactions are interesting because they produce more heat than was needed to get them started in the first place. Here, you only have to add a **SPARK** and all the rest of the **EXPLOSION** is in the chemicals waiting to appear.

The heat produced in this reaction has **two** effects. Firstly, it helps the reaction happen FASTER. Heat makes the **molecules** in the gunpowder **EXCITED** and move around more quickly, meaning they **BASH** into one another more often and **react** more quickly.

Secondly, the heat causes the gases produced by the reacting gunpowder to **expand** SUPERFAST. But the **FIREWORK** is in a sturdy tube, so the gases can only expand in one direction, **down** and **out** – forcing the firework in the **OPPOSITE DIRECTION**, up **HIGH** into the sky.

As the firework **FLIES** high, a second fuse inside the firework continues to **BURN**. This is another TIME-DELAY fuse and ensures the next explosion (**THE BIG, BRIGHT COLOURFUL ONE**) will take place **safely**, way above your heads.

When the burning fuse reaches the second charge, it **IGNITES** another ball of **GUNPOWDER** inside and once again the **rapid expansion** of hot gases flings the contents of this charge burning across the sky in a cascade of **COLOURED SPARKS**.

But gunpowder doesn't have any colour when it **EXPLODES**, otherwise **WAR MOVIES** would look a lot more **FUN**, so the colour is added in by mixing in different chemicals called **'METAL SALTS'**.

Do you remember our old friend the **ELECTRON**? **RUINED** your hair in the morning, got all the other electrons **ANGRY** in the toaster, that electron? Well now, the electron is ready to **pay you back**.

You might remember when molecules had **energy** added, their electrons would **ABSORB** some of it, jump up to a different **ORBIT** away from the nucleus in the middle, and then get **NERVOUS** (not supposed to be there!) spit the extra energy out and drop back down towards the safety of the nucleus again.

The energy which is spat out of fireworks emerges as **VISIBLE LIGHT** and, most **AMAZINGLY**, with different **COLOURS** for different **chemicals**. It's almost like a signature for the chemicals.

COPPER always sends out **BLUE**, **SODIUM** gives off **YELLOW**, **STRONTIUM** is **RED**, **CALCIUM** is **ORANGE** and **BARIUM** will always emit **GREEN**.

When you see these colours **EXPLODING** across the sky, and the crowd is going **OOH!** and **AHH!** you know that it's our **little friend** the **ELECTRON**, putting on an **AMAZING SHOW**.

You can almost **forgive** it for making your **hair** look **SILLY** in the morning.

I Could Sleep
for a Month...

WELL, THAT WAS EXHAUSTING.

You must be ready for a **SLEEP** now, after a day like that. Let's finish where we started then, **BACK IN BED**, drifting through the **PHASES** of sleep, maybe a little **JERK** from your legs as you're drifting off, and then into **deep**, **deep** sleep and dreams of **electrons** and **GIRAFFES** through the **long**, **long** night...

Dream of the future

YAWN and STRETCH. That was a good sleep, wasn't it?

You've never felt so **RESTED**.

It's like you slept for a **HUNDRED YEARS**. You turn over and check the time on your phone and **what?! The date?! YOU DID!** You did sleep for a hundred years!

It's the year **2118**. Or **2119**, depending on when you are reading this book.

(Look, you haven't slept for a hundred years. No one could. Let's just *pretend* you did, and that you woke in the same bed, in the same room, looking exactly the same, but, and this is the important bit, **100 years later...**)

What?

How is this day going to be DIFFERENT?

The bathroom of the future

Well, to start – how about a **NICE SHOWER?** After all, you have one hundred years of **SWEAT** and **EYE GUNK** to get rid of. But this is **no ordinary shower** – this is a **SUPER-EFFICIENT SHOWER** that is able to take water that goes down the drain and **RECYCLE IT**, so that it can come straight back out of the showerhead.

Yes, I know! That sounds **DISGUSTING**. Water you have just used to wash away all the dirt and grease, never mind one hundred years of **dribble** crusted to the side of your mouth, heading down the drain only to come back and **BLAST** you in the face.
NO, THANKS!

But before you turn off the tap in **DISGUST**, know that this shower is similar to the ones already used by **astronauts** on the **International Space Station** to conserve water in space.

Astronauts didn't like the idea of washing their **FACES** in the **SAME WATER** that had just washed their **BOTTOMS** any more than you do, and yet conserving fresh water in space is a **NECESSITY**, as there is no other source for it, other than sending some up by **ROCKET**.

So, the **DRAIN** of this shower isn't like the one in your old shower. It is fitted with **FILTERS** that are able to **EXTRACT** all of the **YUCKY** things in the water so that it is FRESH and **CRYSTAL CLEAR** by the time it comes out of the showerhead again. This shower uses **a tenth** of the water your old shower used and **a fifth** of the energy keeping the water warm.

This might seem a little **extreme**, compared to the life of astronauts. After all, we can usually get **CLEAN** water out of a **TAP** whenever we need it. **BUT** in a hundred years from now, Earth's population will have risen from **7 billion** to more than **11 billion**, and the **DEMAND** for things we take for granted now, like clean water, will be much much **higher**. So, we're going to have to find ways to be more **EFFICIENT**.

Those **POPULATION** changes might have had an **EFFECT** on many more things we take for granted, **such as...**

Time for breakfast

Has sleeping for a hundred years given you an **APPETITE?** **Let's get something to eat.**

YUMMY! Some **sausages** and bacon **rashers!** A favourite. **But** what's that picture on the box? **YUCK!** It looks like **bugs**. Why would they put a picture of **bugs** on your breakfast?

The food we eat might have to change a lot when the population grows to over **11 billion**. One of the **ESSENTIAL** food groups is **PROTEIN**, which we use to build **MUSCLES**. We get a lot of our protein from **MEAT** and **FISH** but...

For every **kilo** of food they produce, **COWS** and **PIGS** need a load of **land** and **WATER** and **feed**. They also produce a lot more gases **(YES, FARTS)** that contribute to **GLOBAL WARMING**. However, and this might take a little getting used to, **FARMING INSECTS** uses less energy and is far **less damaging** to the **ENVIRONMENT** than farming the animals we're more used to.

Bug scientists, called **'entymologists'**, have estimated that at any one time there are approximately **10 quintillion** (that's ten with 18 zeros after it) insects **roaming**, crawling or **BUZZING** around on the planet! For thousands of years, many insects have been part of the **DAILY DIET** of people living in **South America**, **Africa**, **Australia** and **Asia**.

Insects are a **GREAT** source of **PROTEIN** and by farming insects instead, land could be used to grow **FORESTS** which would also absorb some of the excess **carbon dioxide** we burn in our cars.

It's a complete **WIN**.
Insect burger?

All right, we'll give you a **hundred years** to get used to the idea.

So, how else do we feed everyone in **2118**? Well, some scientists believe that the **future** of farming is on, and in, **OCEANS** and **LAKES**. Floating farms, tied to the shore, will grow crops. These crops will bob **up** and **down** on the water's surface. Any **ORGANIC WASTE** from the farm can be used to **FEED** fish kept in pens below. The designers of these floating farms estimate that a single farm measuring just **350 by 200 metres** (1,150 by 650 feet), or about **THREE FOOTBALL PITCHES**, will produce

8 tons of VEGETABLES and almost

2 tons of FISH

every year.

This isn't getting better

Fresh from the lab

Floating farms are great for the **VEGGIES** and **FISHFINGER** eaters of **2118**, and you've already had a bowl of **bugs** for breakfast, but what about some **REAL MEAT?** Is it still possible to get a good **BURGER** or **CHICKEN NUGGETS?**

Yes! Never fear. Your **FAVOURITE** foods are all still available, even though they may never actually have been part of a **LIVING ANIMAL**. Instead, they were grown in a **LABORATORY**.

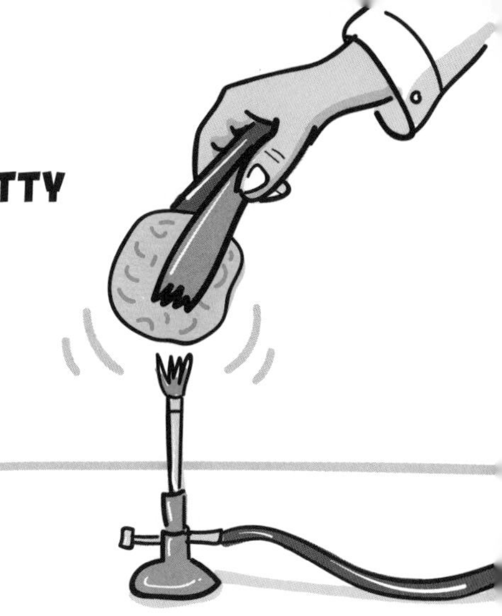

The first ever **HAMBURGER PATTY** created in a lab was made by **scientists** in Maastricht, the Netherlands, and cooked and eaten in **2013**. Muscle cells taken from a living animal are put in a mixture containing special cells that can become any cell in the body, called 'stem cells'. Sort of like a basic **LEGO BRICK**. Also added were food and hormones to help the stem cells **GROW** and **MULTIPLY**. After a few short weeks, the cells reproduce and grow to form strands of **muscle tissue**. That first burger reportedly cost **£220,000** to prepare, but don't forget, one hundred years have passed since then!

The price has dropped so low in **2118** that **EVERYONE** is eating it. **Some people even grow them in their own homes!**

The idea of **lab-grown meat** may take a little bit of getting used to, but there are lots of reasons why it is a BRILLIANT idea. As we said, farm animals need lots of **space** to grow. In 2018, up to **80 per cent** of farmland was used for **farming animals**. A burger produced in a lab would require less than **1 per cent** of the land, so farms can grow more **CROPS**.

Also, lab-grown meat doesn't produce those same gases that contribute to **GLOBAL WARMING**. Basically, lab-grown meat **DOESN'T FART**.

That's **BREAKFAST** (and lunch) covered, so time to make the journey to **school**. Are we still taking a car? Well, **YES**, people who still live on Earth (more on that later) **do** have cars. But they aren't like the ones that were driving around in 2018. For a start, we **don't even drive them any more**. Artificial intelligence (AI) did away with that **ages** ago. You just get in your car, **tell it where to go**, and **spin** your seat around to talk to the other passengers.

Plus, we ran out of **KABOOM** fish juice years ago too. All cars are now **electric** and produce **NO** harmful gases **at all**. Nor do the **POWER STATIONS** that generate the electricity to charge them.

Electricity now comes from **POWER PLANTS** that use the same method of producing energy as the Sun – **NUCLEAR FUSION**.

You've probably heard of nuclear power already. Even in **2018** there were **NUCLEAR POWER STATIONS**. The type of nuclear reaction being used in 2118 is quite **DIFFERENT** though, and a lot **SAFER**.

Back in **2018**, nuclear power stations used **big heavy, heavy URANIUM atoms**. You can see them on the very bottom line of the **PERIODIC TABLE** of elements, as they are so heavy.

In the **reactor** at the heart of the power station, we would fire a stream of **NEUTRONS** (those heavy particles at the centre of an atom) at the uranium atoms and they would **SMASH** apart, breaking into smaller atoms, and releasing lots of heat energy and **SPARE NEUTRONS**. Those spare neutrons then fly off

into the nearby uranium atoms and **SMASH THEM UP**, and so on. This is what we call a **'CHAIN REACTION'**.

It's a bit like if you pushed over a domino but instead of just knocking over **one** domino, it knocked over **two**, and those two knocked over **four** and **so on**. Particularly if all the dominoes released so much heat when they were knocked over that you could eventually **BOIL** a **giant bath** of **WATER**, and use the steam to turn a turbine and make **electricity**.

This is called **'nuclear fission'** (fission means breaking something apart) and it's great for making **ELECTRICITY** because you only have to put a small amount of energy in (those first few neutrons) to get a load more out. To generate the same amount of energy produced by just one gram of **URANIUM** you would need to burn **2 to 3 million** grams of **COAL**, which is **A LOT**. And they are also wonderful because they don't **burn** anything, so other than **WATER VAPOUR** they do not produce gases that contribute to the planet getting **HOTTER**.

So, why didn't we just stick with doing that, eh? **IT SOUNDS PERFECT!**

Yeah, there are some problems.

The easiest things to break apart tend to be the really **huge** atoms, like **URANIUM**, and they are already pretty unstable because they are so **BIG**. They spend their time trying to get **smaller** and more stable, and they do this by spitting out particles from the central section, **THE NUCLEUS**.

It's as if you were sitting on a chair with just too many **cushions**, but as you settled down you realized you weren't totally **COMFORTABLE** so you took one of the cushions and threw it across the room and tried settling down again. But it still wasn't **JUST** right so you threw another cushion across the room. And you just keep **THROWING** those cushions across the room until you're **finally comfortable**.

Similarly, some types of **URANIUM** just can't settle down and keep flinging out particles until the nucleus is **stable**. The types of particles thrown out by **URANIUM** is called '**RADIATION**', which is **very**, **very DANGEROUS** to humans. Radiation can travel through our skin and damage the **DNA** in our cells and make us very ill just like sunlight. And uranium keeps throwing out these really **DANGEROUS** particles for **THOUSANDS** of years.

So, even though **URANIUM** is really **USEFUL**, it is really **DANGEROUS** and stays **really DANGEROUS** for a **long**, **long** time. We must take all sorts of **PRECAUTIONS** with it to keep ourselves **SAFE**, like burying it in concrete. Even then we even have to worry about **UNCONTROLLABLE** things like earthquakes, in case they cause leaks of **RADIOACTIVITY** that will make a region unsafe to live in for centuries.

So, yes, some problems.

So, what has changed in **2118?**

We've stopped doing nuclear **fission**. Now, we're all about nuclear **FUSION!**

'**FUSION**' means pushing things together and, back in **2018** it was just a great unproven idea. Thankfully, by 2118, scientists have **WORKED OUT** the problems **(we hope)!**

FUSION is **better** than **fission** because rather than breaking big (unstable, radioactive, dangerous) things apart, we're SQUEEZING small (stable, non-radioactive, safe) things together. Specifically, types of **hydrogen**, the **lightest** of all of the elements (floating waaay above nasty, heavy uranium in the periodic table), which can be found in normal, old **SEAWATER**. And we have **loads** of that.

So, safe power for all!

It's just a **PITY** we didn't invent it **EARLIER...**

Too late!

Unfortunately, scientists didn't harness the power of **NUCLEAR FUSION** quickly enough. Generations of burning **FOSSIL FUELS** proved too much for the world's climate.

Burning **FOSSIL FUELS**, all those compressed **DEAD FISH**, produces gases that stop heat from the Sun **ESCAPING** back into **SPACE**. Another gas that does this is **methane**, which is one of the gases found in the **FARTS** of all those hundreds of millions of **COWS** and **PIGS** we've been farming.

These gases float up to form a layer **HIGH** up in the Earth's **ATMOSPHERE** that acts like the **GLASS** on a greenhouse. Heat from the sun reaches the surface of the planet but a lot of it is supposed to be

REFLECTED back into space. Instead, these gases **TRAP** the heat, causing the **TEMPERATURE** of the planet to rise.

For the last 150 years or so, we humans have been producing far more of those gases than ever before, multiplying this greenhouse effect all that time.

We can see the long-term effects of the greenhouse effect gone mad on **Venus,** where greenhouses gases have helped the temperature rise to **460°C** (860°F), making it the **HOTTEST** planet in the **Solar System**.

The effect on Earth is not quite as **DRAMATIC** as that, but we might see many changes over the next **100 years** as the temperature rises.

Hooray! Long hot summers!

Yes and no. A lot of places might get a lot hotter, but instead of **SUNNIER** holidays, the world is going to have to work a lot harder to provide **FOOD** and **fresh water** to feed everyone and they will have to do this with **less land**, and with **crops** that aren't used to growing at these temperatures and might not give us as much food.

More sea!

The **WARMER TEMPERATURES** cause much of the ice at the poles to **MELT** causing the sea levels to rise. This means lots of places you might have liked to go to on holiday in **2018** are **BELOW** the ocean in **2118**. Famous destinations like Miami or Venice might be below the waves in a century.

More sand!

The warmer **TEMPERATURES** will also cause the deserts to expand. Areas that were once able to farm food are vast dust bowls unable to grow crops or rear livestock in **2118**.

The extra **TEMPERATURE** also means there's **loads** more **energy** in the atmosphere, so there are **STRONGER** winds and more **STORMS** and just heaps more **CRAZY** weather generally.

It's no wonder that by **2118** humans have set their sights further afield.

Life on Mars

In **2118**, people are living **QUITE HAPPILY** on **Mars**. After the first couple of trips by humans, we got very **SMART** and sent **ROBOTS** up to prepare the place for us.

These **ROBOTS** set to work building a colony that people would be able to live in. When they were done **BUILDING HOMES**, **SAFE POWER** and **FOOD SUPPLIES**, the people followed. At first, they just came as tourists, but then miners arrived and the **EXPLORERS**. Then people were needed to look after all these constant arrivals and those people needed **homes**, **hospitals**, **schools** for their children and places to have fun, and so the building **CONTINUED**. Mars is **LOVELY** now. **Just you wait!**

Sure, there isn't a **BEACH**, or a **POOL**, or much water at all, but every night, the **ROBOTS** hold a huge **FIREWORKS SHOW**. **Blue** and **green** and **yellow** against the night sky. It makes a nice change from all the **red**.

It does take about **A YEAR** to get there, **BUT** the view is

AMAZING, particularly at the start and the end of the journey. Just look out of the window as you **HURTLE** away from Earth.

The **continents** look a little different now since the sea levels have risen. Sure, there are no **ICY WHITE BITS** at the top and bottom any more, and a bit more **DESERT** here and there.

BUT IT'S STILL A BEAUTIFUL SIGHT.

And soon you'll have a **whole new planet** to investigate.

What will a normal day be like on Mars?

You'll have to wait and see when you wake up in 2118.

Only a few more sleeps to go...

We Need
Your Help

Hey! Do you remember this face?

We could have used that **face** the whole way through that last chapter. **Nuclear Fission**, **FLIGHTS TO MARS**, **LAB-GROWN MEAT**, right now they would **all** get this face from scientists.

But that's the whole point, isn't it? It's about being **CONFUSED** by something and wanting to **understand** it and then, hopefully, asking the **right question** to find the answer. So, if we're really lucky, in **a hundred years' time**, we can sit on Mars and watch the fireworks go off.

But that's a lot of different **questions**, being asked by a lot of different people.

Right at the **START** of the book I said that if there was something in here you found **less interesting**, then you should feel free to skip ahead to the bits you **LIKED** more.

There were a couple of reasons for this.

Firstly, this is what adults do **ALL** the time. Next time your dad picks up a newspaper and immediately turns to the **SPORTS PAGES**, you can give him a look like, **"I see what you're doing there."**

And secondly, because, when it comes to **science** and **CURIOSITY**, actually we don't expect anyone to be curious about

EVERYTHING. It's a funny thing about humans. We all like to **SPECIALIZE**; to dig down into the things we really love, to **DISCOVER** our passion for a small corner of a subject that we make all our own.

And, hey! We're just going to keep **dangling** different subjects in front of you until you find the one that just makes you go, "**AHA!** Now, that's the stuff I like!"

So, if you were really **INTERESTED** in exactly how those **EXPLODING FISH** make the cars work, then you might be interested in **engines**, and guess what, that makes you an **ENGINEER**.

Although there are **loads** of different types of engineers...

If you want to know how **WINGS WORK** you'd be an **aeronautical engineer**.

I like taking apart as much as building

Maybe it was the **ACCELEROMETERS** that make VR work? An **electronic engineer**.

Of course, engineers aren't the only scientists. If it was the **ELECTRONS** and the **WAVES** and the **ELECTROMAGNETIC** spectrum that did it for you, maybe you're a **physicist**.

If you liked the **MOLECULES**, you might be a **chemist**.

If you like asking questions about how the brain works, you might be a **neuroscientist**.

If you're more interested in the **body**, and **HORMONES**, and **EARS POPPING**, and **SLEEP**, and all that **squelchy** stuff about what's inside us, you might be a **doctor**, or an **anatomist**, or a **physiologist**.

If you're interested in all that **MEDICAL STUFF**, but especially when it comes to food and how the body uses it, you might be a **DIETICIAN**.

Was it the giraffes that got you? **You could be a zoologist**.

These are all separate jobs, done by different people (and there are so many, many more), and in each of those jobs there are people who look like **this:**

People are still asking **QUESTIONS** in each of these subjects, and there are still many things to discover. So, find your **FAVOURITE** area and ask all the questions you can think of. And by the

time you've found those **answers**, I guarantee you'll have **even more questions**.

Or **maybe**, just **maybe**, you liked it **ALL**.

Maybe you found it all equally interesting.

Maybe you have a **CURIOSITY** so **huge** that, just for now you'd like to carry on **LEARNING** about all these things.

In which case, **maybe** you could become the most **AMAZING SCIENTIST** we have, drawing on all the **knowledge** in the world, to solve the

BIGGEST QUESTION OF ALL...

How DO we make the best sandcastle?
GOOD LUCK!

About the author

DARA Ó BRIAIN

Dara Ó Briain has a degree in **Mathematics and Mathematical Physics** from University College Dublin. As well as being a **FAMOUS** stand-up **COMEDIAN**, he is one of the BBC's best-known faces of science, presenting such shows as **Dara Ó Briain's Science Club**, flagship astronomy show **Stargazing Live** and DARA Ó BRIAIN: SCHOOL OF HARD SUMS. He lives in London, owns a **TELESCOPE** and has a photo of himself with **Buzz Aldrin**, of which he is **very** PROUD.

His first book for children is

Beyond the Sky: You and the Universe.

Scientific notes

INDEX

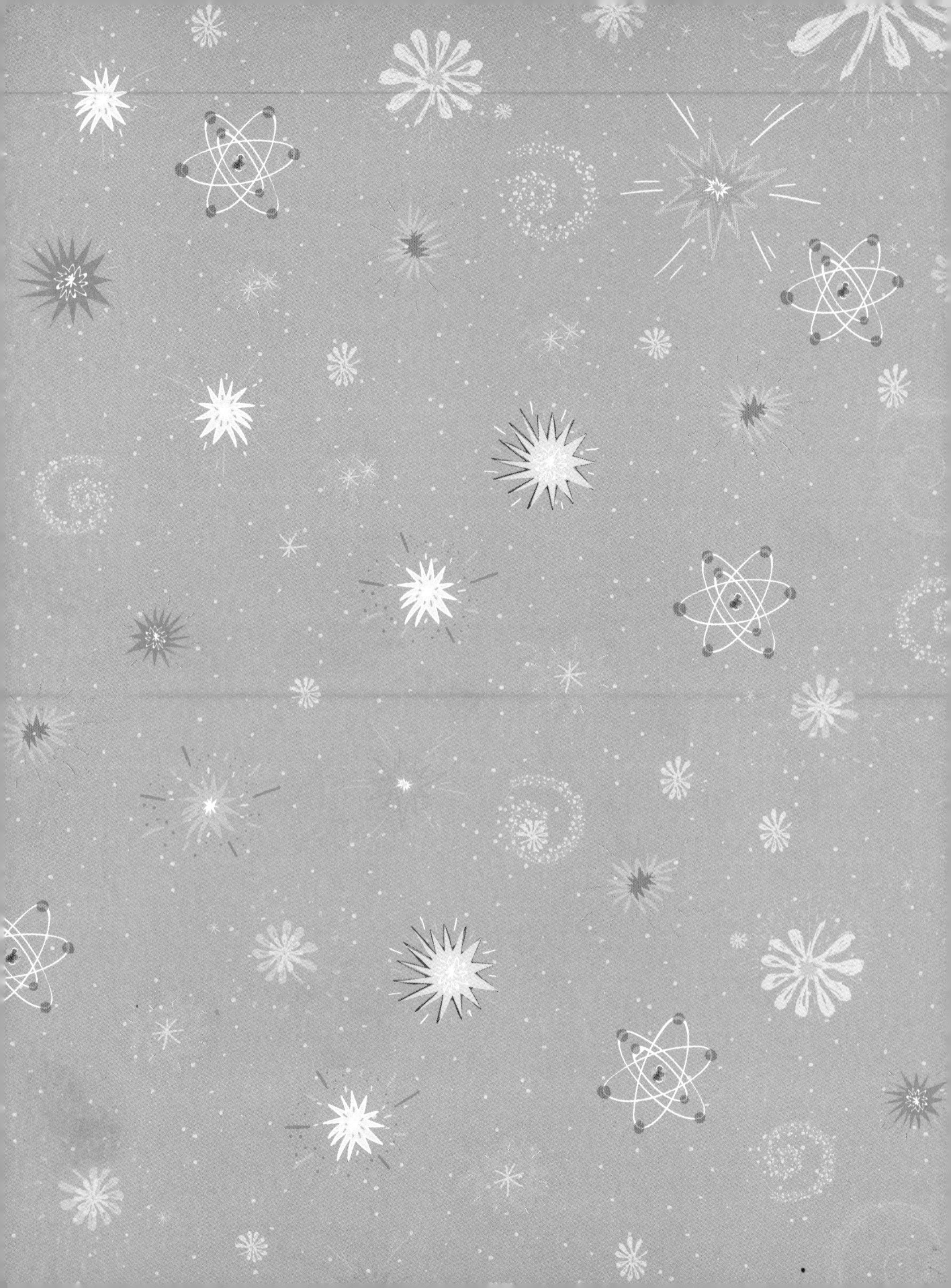